PENGUIN ANANDA

TH

Gauranga Das is a lea[...]sed in Mumbai. A graduate from [...]mbay, he found his calling to be[...] Governing Body Commission at Intern[...] Society for Krishna Consciousness (ISKCON), he is actively involved in enhancing leadership effectiveness and governance of temples and communities globally. He is dedicated to helping people transform their hearts, establish sustainable and spiritual communities, and drive a positive change in society. A multifaceted spiritualist on a mission to create a value-based society, he is a mindful meditation expert, strategic character educationist, sustainability and climate change warrior and social welfare catalyst.

He is the director of ISKCON's Govardhan Ecovillage (GEV), founded by Radhanath Swami. The GEV, representing India, has won over thirty-six national and international awards, including the UN World Tourism Organization (UNWTO) Award in 2017 for its innovative model of 'Eco-Tourism as a Catalyst for Rural Development'. Gauranga Das has also strategized and led the execution of GEV's synergistic solution for Sustainable Development Goals for climate change and enabled GEV's accreditation to multiple UN bodies such as UNEP, UN ECOSOC, UNCCD and UNCBD. He is UNEP's Faith for Earth Councillor on behalf of ISKCON. The Indian Green Building Council (IGBC) has recognized him as an IGBC fellow for his contribution to the green building movement.

He sits on the board of the Govardhan School of Public Leadership, an institution that prepares students for the civil services exam. He has led several youth empowerment initiatives across the world to successfully inculcate in them clarity of purpose, purity of character and compassion in relationships. He is also the administrative director of the Bhaktivedanta Research Center (BRC), an initiative of ISKCON to connect professionals, housewives and students to the academic study of philosophy, create libraries of Vedic literatures and manuscripts, and facilitate MA and PhD programmes in philosophy.

Celebrating 35 Years of
Penguin Random House India

ADVANCE PRAISE FOR THE BOOK

'Gauranga Das Prabhu has been a spiritual mentor to me. There are very few souls in this world who have dedicated as much time and attention to the study of scriptures. There are even fewer who are able to intricately explain the nuances of scriptural wisdom in simple words. I've always believed that Prabhuji's purpose is to spread the unfiltered teachings of Krishna to the souls of the modern day. Any work of his is a must-read if you're on a quest for ancient wisdom. This book is no exception! A must-read for anyone trying to navigate life's uncertainties with a warrior's mindset'—Ranveer Allahbadia, social media entrepreneur, YouTuber and leadership coach

'For a singer, *riyaaz* [practice] is at the core of building proficiency. It needs to become a habit no matter how proficient one has become. It's not easy to cultivate good habits. But a scholar like Gauranga Das ji, has helped us readers with tips through powerful storytelling in simple language so that we don't just read this but apply the learning in life'—Kailash Kher, music composer and singer

'It's a delightful work by Prabhu Ji, a breezy read, a book woven with stories and anecdotes that tend to linger long after one has read it. The narratives are real and very believable and address today's complex problems with a lucid voice and simple gaze. Without being preachy, they prescribe profound solutions through age-old wisdom distilled for our times'—Himanshu Gautam, CEO, Safalta.com

'Gauranga Prabhu has a knack for conveying deep life philosophy in a modern-day context. This, combined with empathy for what today's youth grapple with day in, day out, is this handbook for life. *The Art of Habits* is a must-have for every young, ambitious Indian who wants to constantly get better while consistently delivering impactful results, both in personal and professional life'—Bhimaraya Metri, director, Indian Institute of Management, Nagpur

THE art OF HABITS

40 STORIES *to* uplift the mind *and* transform the heart

GAURANGA DAS

PENGUIN
ANANDA

An imprint of Penguin Random House

PENGUIN ANANDA

USA | Canada | UK | Ireland | Australia
New Zealand | India | South Africa | China | Singapore

Penguin Ananda is part of the Penguin Random House group of companies
whose addresses can be found at global.penguinrandomhouse.com

Published by Penguin Random House India Pvt. Ltd
4th Floor, Capital Tower 1, MG Road,
Gurugram 122 002, Haryana, India

First published in Penguin Ananda by Penguin Random House India 2023

10 9 8 7 6 5 4 3 2 1

ISBN 9780143452751

Typeset in Adobe Caslon Pro by Manipal Technologies Limited, Manipal

www.penguin.co.in

MIX
Paper from
responsible sources
FSC® C010615

Contents

When Good Fortune Arises

Human Quality: Obedience

Once in the holy town of Pandharpur, there lived a saintly person, Sant Narayan, who preached the chanting of the holy names of Lord Vitthala, a deity form of Lord Krishna. Pandharpur is a well-known pilgrimage town on the banks of Chandrabhaga River, in the Solapur district of Maharashtra. It is home to the glorious Vitthala-Rukmini temple that attracts about a million Hindu pilgrims during the month of *Ashadh* (June–July).

It is said that Shri Krishna came to Pandharpur to meet his disciple Bhakta Pundalika, who was busy serving his parents at that moment. He offered a brick (called *viṭ* in Marathi) to Shri Krishna and requested him to be seated on it while he attended to his parents. Shri Krishna has been waiting on that brick for the last twenty-eight *yuga*s (eras) and thus he is also known as Vitthala.

It was a hot forenoon in May and Sant Narayan, as part of his preaching efforts, went around the town singing glories of Lord Vitthala. He engaged in conversations with people, inquiring about their well-being and sharing the benefits of chanting the holy name in the age of Kali. That day, Sant Narayan reached out to a farmer, explaining the process and benefits of chanting the holy names to him. The farmer refused to listen to him, saying he was busy at the farm. Not being insistent, the saint blessed him, wished him well and moved on. Their paths crossed again a month later and yet again, the saint preached to the farmer, who didn't lend him an ear a second time.

They met a third time in the holy month of Ashadh, and that too on the *Ekadashi* day. Ekadashi, the eleventh day of a Vedic month, is considered auspicious for devotees of Krishna. And in the month of Ashadh, Ekadashi is considered the holiest day in the temple town of Pandharpur. This day, a huge *yatra* or religious procession of pilgrims known as the Ashadi Ekadasi Waari Yatra culminates at Pandharpur. Devotees take *padayatra* (journey by foot) from different parts of the state for a *darshan* (auspicious viewing) of Lord Vitthala on this day. When Sant Narayan chanced upon the farmer, he walked up to him and spoke about the glories of Ekadashi and requested him to chant the holy name to please Lord Vitthala.

'Swamiji, I have no time,' the farmer responded. 'Practically all my time goes in farming.'

'OK, if you do not have time to chant the holy names, at least try to visit the temple once in a while.'

'The temple is far from my home,' the farmer replied. 'And I will have to walk several kilometres to go there. It is not possible.'

This exchange continued and no matter the suggestion Sant Narayan made, the farmer replied in the negative, making all kinds of excuses.

Finally, with great patience, the saint folded his hands and said, 'My dear young man, I heard a list of things you cannot do. Now I want to ask you, is there something you can do?'

The farmer thought for some time, and said, 'Yes, I have a neighbour, Gopal, who is a potter. And what I can do is that in the morning, I can first see him, and only after seeing him will I eat my food. This is something I can do.'

'All right,' the saint said, 'go ahead and do this; make this your first regulation in life.'

The farmer began to follow this regulation daily. He would climb up on the fence of his house and see the potter at his wheel every morning. Once he had seen him, the farmer would have his breakfast. This became a daily routine. The farmer felt satisfied that he had managed to keep his word to the saint. More than a month passed this way.

One day, the farmer had to leave for the fields earlier than usual. It was well before time, and when he climbed on the fence, the potter was not to be seen. The farmer grew worried. 'How will I eat my food today? I'm feeling hungry, I must leave now as well,' he thought.

So, he jumped across the fence and rushed towards the potter's usual seat. He realized that the potter had left the wheel. Walking a few paces ahead, he saw that the potter was at another spot in his backyard, digging mud for his pottery work.

Just then, while digging the mud, the potter chanced upon a pot underground. It contained gold, rubies, emeralds and jewels. The potter was astonished. His first thought was to check if someone had seen him uncover this pot of fine jewels. He got up, looked around and saw the farmer pacing towards him. At that moment, he became anxious.

As soon as the farmer caught sight of the potter, he was thrilled because he had fulfilled the rules and regulations for that day, and kept his word to the saint. But the potter turned away immediately and started to walk back.

As the potter saw the farmer run away, he got suspicious and cried out, 'Hey, what happened?'

'I saw you, I saw you,' the farmer responded in a state of joy.

The potter became even more suspicious and asked, 'What did you see here?'

'You don't need to know that. I saw you.'

This bewildered the potter, and he feared that the farmer had seen him with the pot of jewels. It further added to his anxiety when he wondered whether the farmer would let the whole town know of all the jewels in the pot. This could very well land him in a dispute and possibly strip him of his lucky possession.

Without waiting any further, the potter ran up to the farmer and stopped him.

'Hey!' the potter patted the farmer on the shoulder. 'Hold on a minute.'

'What happened?!' the farmer exclaimed.

'Look, I know you saw me . . .' the potter confessed and showed him the pot. 'Do you want any of these jewels?'

The farmer was astonished and couldn't quite fathom what was happening right in front of his eyes.

'I will give you 50 per cent of what I have.'

'What?' the dazed farmer replied.

'Yes, I will. But please don't let the town know about it,' the potter warned.

It took a few seconds for the farmer to come to terms with reality because the jewels in the pot were worth more than anything he could possibly earn if he farmed for the rest of his life. As he deliberated the potter's proposal, a powerful thought struck him.

The farmer realized that if following this simple regulation of the saint could land him a pot of jewels worth more than his lifetime earnings, what could he achieve by truly following the words of that great soul—by chanting the holy name of Krishna.

In the *Srimad Bhagavatam* (3.24.13), it is said:

> *etāvaty eva śuśrūṣā*
> *kāryā pitari putrakaiḥ*
> *bāḍham ity anumanyeta*
> *gauraveṇa guror vacaḥ*

It is the duty of each one of us to fulfil the desires of great souls, the pure devotees of the Lord, get their sanction, permission and blessings. The powerful energy and force created through those blessings cause a total transformation in our lives. We must experience it in order to understand the power of obedience.

Following the words of the great souls is a step towards attaining the greatest fortune, the mercy of God. The good fortune of the Lord's mercy is rare. To attain it, we must understand and inculcate certain exalted qualities exhibited by the great souls, so that we can attempt to attract and please the Lord.

Here are three things that can help us earn the mercy of the Supreme Lord.

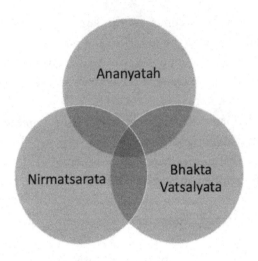

ANANYATAH—FOCUSED DETERMINATION EARNS THE LORD'S LOVE

Krishna affirms Arjuna that one who is on the path of devotion must have Ananya Bhakti towards the Lord. The focused determination to please Him is the first principle one has to follow. When the Kurukshetra battle was announced and both parties started forming allies, Duryodhana and Arjuna were converging in Dwaraka to seek the support of the Yadu dynasty. This was a highly tempting situation for Arjuna, an entire army from Dwaraka could be his, yet he didn't care for such material fortune. When Duryodhana opted for the opulence of the Narayani army, he thought the material prospect would add strength to his army. Arjuna chose his dear friend Krishna instead. Although he had a deck of choices in front of him, he chose the unalloyed shelter of Krishna because he put all of his faith in Him. He didn't desire anything but the loving friendship of the Lord. Funnily, Duryodhana thought Arjuna was too sentimental and impractical.

BHAKTA VATSALYATA—LOYALTY IS RECIPROCATED BY PROTECTION

Arjuna was extremely loyal to Krishna and so was Krishna to Arjuna. Just as we hold those most precious to us close to our hearts, similarly, Krishna was highly protective of the Pandavas and Draupadi. He was willing to protect them at all costs; he even took the menial position of a charioteer for Arjuna's cart. In those days, the warriors would kick the back of the charioteers to give directions. Indeed, Arjuna kicked the Supreme Personality of Godhead according to the direction he wanted the cart to take. When the Lord sacrifices himself for his loving devotee, he is called Bhakta Vatsala. Although the Pandavas made several mistakes, Krishna was patient and tolerant and continued to help them through adversities. Such a position is earned with sincere dedication to the service of one's spiritual master and the Lord. As practising *sadhaka*s (those who follow a spiritual path), we slowly learn to love God. The Lord's heart melts to the extent that he stays extremely tolerant and patient with our immature yet sincere attempts to please him.

NIRMATSARATA—KRISHNA IS PLEASED BY NON-ENVIOUSNESS

Arjuna and the rest of the Pandavas possessed a unique quality called *nirmatsarata*, meaning being completely non-envious. Arjuna was the third eldest of the five Pandavas.

When Krishna became Arjuna's chariot driver, the other brothers could have easily protested. Yudhisthira didn't think he deserved Krishna's help as the eldest. Bhima, too, didn't demand that Krishna be with him, since he was the most powerful of them all. Nakula and Sahadev did not protest either. Each one could have made a logical argument but none of them asked Krishna to stay with them even for a day. This was because of their pure love and selfless adoration for another Vaishnava who received the Lord's mercy. Such were the benevolent hearts of the pure devotees of the Lord.

The Supreme Lord is very selective in granting his mercy because he yields easily to the love of his devotees. In the Mahabharata, Krishna performed many sacrifices and was always protecting the family of the Pandavas whenever they helplessly took the Lord's shelter. By pleasing the Vaishnavas and cultivating the qualities above with humility and servitude, one can easily satisfy the Supreme Lord, Shri Krishna.

TWO

Moments That Matter

Human Quality: Tolerance

It was a hot, humid morning in June in the city of Mumbai. One of the hottest days of the decade, the mercury touched 43 degrees Celsius. The local trains are the lifeline of this city of dreams, truly, the mode of transport for all seasons! Weekday mornings and evenings are when they are most crowded with officegoers commuting between their workplace and home.

On the Western Line, the trains run between Churchgate and Borivali, about 80 km apart. The commotion is at its peak in Dadar as the alighting and boarding of passengers happen at breakneck speed within a few seconds of the train halting. One such morning, Yogesh, a middle-aged officegoer, managed to sneak his way into a jam-packed general compartment as the train halted at Dadar. He was one of the 1000 people crammed in a compartment with a standard capacity of 400. Dressed in a simple cotton shirt and trousers, carrying a shoulder bag, he was pacing himself few centimetres at a time, jostling for space inside the compartment. He was all smiles, in appreciation of fellow travellers and their attitude to go through so much strenuousness to earn a livelihood and make ends meet for their family. It was so crowded in that compartment that it was difficult for him to even find the breathing space.

Crushed between people on all directions, his face was pressed against the shoulder of the man in front. There was a jerk and by the law of inertia, his body moved to eventually push the man in front. The man turned back in anger. He was giant, dressed in a kurta, with as many as eight rings decorating his fingers, the thumbs spared, and a hefty chain around his neck. Chewing paan, he looked at Yogesh intensely. Just then, there was another jerk and Yogesh inadvertently stepped on this man's toes, Yogesh's boots on top of his slippers. The man shrieked in pain. He lost his temper within moments and slapped Yogesh on his left cheek.

The profusely sweating crowd turned to them. People anticipated a fierce response and gathered to avert a tense situation in a coach with absolutely no room (pun intended) for it.

'Did you slap me in anger or as a joke?' asked a smiling Yogesh.

This big, powerful, hefty man had the shock of his life. 'What?' he blurted out. 'I slapped you in anger. What will you do?'

'Well, nothing,' Yogesh said. 'Just that I don't like jokes.'

This dampened the tense situation. Every person around them was surprised yet relieved.

So many times, we are faced with situations in life where there is a provocation, and that provocation may force us to react immediately. But before we do that, we should evaluate whether we have the capacity to overcome that situation.

When we are provoked we have two alternatives—to retaliate or to tolerate it—and we must make a call depending on the seriousness of the situation. It would be foolish to underestimate the situation and try to react aggressively at a time when we may not have the capacity to do so. Sometimes it is better to wait for the situation to change, to tolerate it in the present so that we can be in a stronger position in future. Therefore, to retaliate instantly is not always good, sometimes tolerance pays off.

The third verse of the *siksastaka* prayers of Chaitanya Mahaprabhu is:

tṛṇād api sunīcena
taror api sahiṣṇunā
amāninā mānadena
kīrtanīyaḥ sadā hariḥ

One should be more tolerant than the tree, devoid of all sense of false prestige and ready to offer all respect to others. In such a state of mind one can chant the holy name of the Lord constantly.

Further, in the Mahabharata, Shri Bhishmadeva talks about the following benefits of cultivating tolerance:

1. **Through tolerance one can conquer desires and avarice**
   Tolerance is not just a virtue that controls external behaviour, it is a path to mindfulness. When we nurture a culture of tolerance, we gain control over the mind and we can take stock of situations calmly. When the wants of the mind are unchecked, they can wreak havoc by inducing

arrogance and unruly behaviour. It is said that an intolerant person is typically dogmatic with a closed mind. On the other side, a tolerant person with a controlled mind is broad-minded and more collaborative. Such a person can conquer not just their desires but their avarice too.

2. **Through self-control we can be free of false hopes**

    Tolerance cements acceptance of a given situation in the mind, specifically when it's unfavourable. Acceptance is a sign of humility, where the individual accepts the will of God as overarching. They know that the efforts that they put in and their talent are a minuscule part of the whole and that they alone don't shape the outcomes in any situation in life. A tolerant person, in that sense, is realistic; they neither give room to false hopes nor are they adamant to pursue that which is beyond their reach.

3. **Through the practice of yoga one can control the body**

    Of all the senses, the tongue and genitals are considered the most volatile. Yoga involves meditation and a focused attempt to stabilize the mind and the body. The timeless Vedic scriptures describe how controlling them is key to success in life. The word yoga is derived from the Sanskrit root word *yuj*, meaning 'to unite'. The practice of yoga aims to create union between body, mind and spirit, as well as between the individual self and universal consciousness. Such a union tends to neutralize ego-driven thoughts and behaviours, creating a sense of spiritual awakening in the individual. This begins with tolerance, when the mind is in a state of control and receptive to the voice of the soul.

4. **False arguments can be conquered by factual assertion**

   When one is tolerant, the mind is more stable. With that equipoise, they are able to reason logically and can assess the validity of various arguments. Most importantly, they are not devoured by the impulsive behaviour arising from the false ego. As a result, they logically analyse the situation in light of the available facts without getting swayed by sentiment. Even if they know they are on the back foot or if they have to make an unfavourable decision, they don't desist. A tolerant mind sides with what is fair.

5. **Exercising tolerance in speech is the path to greatness**

   The tongue not only craves to eat but to speak as well. We may be able to develop control over ourselves so that we do not physically harm anyone but we are quite careless when it comes to non-violence in words. It is said that the tongue is sharper than a sword. A wound caused by a sword may heal, but the wound from someone's words breaking our heart might not. A tolerant person is better placed when it comes to exercising caution in speech by keeping silence when provoked. In fact, the founder *acharya* of the ISKCON Society, Srila Prabhupada says, 'The greatness of a person lies in his ability to tolerate provoking situations'.

THREE

Conquering Grudges

Human Quality: Conflict Management

Naina and Nikhil, a newly married couple, lived in a multi-storeyed apartment in Ayodhya Nagar, Bhopal. Nikhil led a thriving business, a chain of supermarkets spread across the city, while Naina worked as teacher at a CBSE school.

It had been two months since their wedding and as they began to get to know each other better after their arranged marriage, married life also made way for frequent tiffs between them. It was a pleasant February evening and the couple had been battling a quarrel since forenoon. Although the tension had begun to ease, they remained moody. Nikhil proposed that they go for a drive as a breath of fresh air that spring evening could calm things down. Though Naina preferred privacy, she reluctantly agreed to go with him.

Nikhil was driving, and after passing through central business districts on to the national highway, he began to speed up. He decided to revisit the core issue of the spat that afternoon, to put forth his points with an intention to resolve the conflict. Naina was not keen on a discussion just then, Nikhil's points provoked her. The exchange went on for a while, only to metamorphose into an argument again. Matters turned worse and Naina was both pensive and angry. With no further talk, there was absolute silence in the car. In an attempt to vent his pent-up anger, Nikhil pressed the accelerator and the car sped up.

After a few more kilometres, a cop overtook the car and signalled Nikhil to stop. Nikhil obeyed and parked the car in the side lane. He got down.

The cop walked up to Nikhil, 'Hey, why are you speeding like this?'

'Sir, but . . .' Nikhil uttered in anguish, 'Sir, actually I was driving within the speed limit but I may have sped at the last moment.'

'Do you know what speed you were driving at?'

At this point, Naina came out of the car.

'I don't know, sir,' Nikhil pleaded. 'Please forgive me.'

'He always speeds up beyond 100 kmph,' Naina chimed in, disgust writ all over her face.

Nikhil ground his teeth in anger.

'You were speeding at 110 kmph,' the cop confirmed.

'I always tell him to drive slow, he never listens to me.'

Now the cop looked at Nikhil with suspicion.

'Well,' the cop continued, 'I see that the tail light is broken.'

'Actually, just last week, I hit against the post and the tail light broke.'

'I have been telling you for the last two weeks,' Naina added, 'to fix that tail light, you never listen to me.'

'Naina,' Nikhil retorted in a low tone, 'will you just shut up?'

'Sir,' the cop picked up a new issue, 'I don't think you were wearing a seatbelt while driving.'

'I saw that you were approaching me, and just then, I removed the seatbelt,' Nikhil responded.

Nikhil was praying Naina wouldn't utter a word then. But she did.

'I keep telling him all the time to wear the seatbelt but you well know, he never listens to me.'

The cop was astonished to see the issue play out this way.

Furious now, Nikhil yelled at Naina, 'Will you just shut up and stop making up these stories?'

The cop looked at them both and then asked Naina, 'Does your husband always behave like this?'

Naina looked at Nikhil for a moment and told the cop, 'No, sir.'

Just when Nikhil began to feel relieved, she completed the sentence, 'Only when he is drunk, he behaves like this.'

It is said:

> *aparādha-sahasrāṇi*
> *kriyante 'har-niṣaṁ mayā*
> *dāso 'ham iti māṁ matvā*
> *kṣamasva madhusūdana*

'I commit thousands of offenses day and night. But, thinking of me as Your servant, kindly forgive those, O Madhusūdana [Kṛṣṇa].'

So many times, we carry grudges in our heart; a grudge is like acid. The first damage the acid does is to the very pot in which it is carried. Therefore, we should realize that it is best to overcome grudges for a peaceful life. Firstly, it's important to understand that none of us can remain alone, we need each other, we always coexist. Secondly, we need to realize that nobody is born perfect, people have imperfections. Thirdly, we should become aware that in every situation there could be a possible misunderstanding that is circumstantial and we should be willing to overlook it.

Conflicts are a regular feature in this world of constant interactions influenced by the modes of material nature, especially passion and ignorance.

When two parties try to resolve a conflict the following four principles may help:

1. Sincere Confession

Sincere intent to overcome one's bad habits which have caused the conflict is the first step. This reflects the person's intent to resolve the conflict. However, if one has no genuine intention to rectify one's mistakes but puts up a façade and ritualistically utters the often abused five letter word (sorry), then one is a sinner.

2. Clarification versus Justification

One may clarify the circumstances and intentions behind the unpleasant deed. This should be followed by an apology for any inadvertent hurting of someone's feelings. Denying one's faults and justifying one's deeds by rationalizing will do no good to forge trust and will prove counterproductive.

3. Offence after Apology

An apology holds no value if the mistakes committed are not innocent or circumstantial. If they stem from one's prolonged and deep-rooted envy or anger towards others, it makes matters worse. Repeating the same mistake after apologizing hurts the credibility of the person and doesn't quite help in building bridges for relationships to thrive.

4. Sincerity in Apology

It's often said, 'Say what you mean and mean what you say'. If one's apology is not sincere, it often shows. They may pretend to say sorry successfully at that moment, but their actions over time expose them. Actions do speak louder than words and their say-to-do ratio will stand the test of time.

FOUR

My Voice Matters

Human Quality: Pride

It was a bright, sunny morning in the city of Mangaluru in coastal Karnataka. It was the onset of spring and the flowers had just begun to bloom. In the hope of getting alms, a beggar made his way to a residential area. He wore a faded lungi, his starving stomach looked withered and a couple of remaining teeth were stained brown from betel chewing. He had pink, peeling blisters on his bare feet which needed a pair of slippers to combat the forenoon heat.

He knocked at the gate of a palatial, independent house and called, 'Amma, Amma, help me.'

After a few seconds, out came a young lady clad in salwar kameez. Standing at the entrance, she stared at him for a moment.

His eyes lit up and he begged again, 'Amma, Amma, help me.'

'Get lost,' she shouted in a shrill, inhumane tone. 'Earn yourself, I have nothing to give you.'

The beggar was taken aback, but he pleaded with her yet again, 'Please give me something at least.'

'No, absolutely nothing, get out!' she said firmly and shut the door.

Feeling desolate, the beggar began to walk away from the house. As he took a few steps on the road, another lady opened the gate and walked into the house. She was dressed in a saree and looked much older than the one he had spoken to earlier. He sensed that she must be the senior member of the family. Not giving up hope yet, he thought of asking for her help.

'Amma, Amma, please help,' he began.

The elder lady stopped for a moment and stared at him.

'Madam,' he tried something new in the hope of a positive reaction, 'do you know what happened just now?'

'What happened?' she asked.

'The lady in this house . . .' he started.

'My daughter-in law, you mean?'

'Yes, ma'am,' he quickly confirmed, after realizing that she was indeed the young woman's mother-in-law. 'I begged for some donation, but she didn't even care to listen and shut the door right away.'

'Is it so?' the lady asked, riled up.

'Yes, how can this happen in such a good family?' the beggar tried to please her, sensing a window of opportunity.

'OK, please come with me,' she ordered.

Gleaming, the beggar followed the lady to the entrance.

'Stay here,' she said in a raised voice to grab her daughter-in-law's attention.

Within moments, the mother-in-law yelled at the beggar, 'Get lost!'

This bewildered him.

'Amma?' he questioned her in shock.

'I said, get lost!'

'You brought me here again for this?'

'Well,' the mother-in-law retorted with an eye on the daughter-in-law, 'this house belongs to me, and I have the first right and power to decide.'

The beggar was shocked and decided never to step near that house again.

The mother-in-law's final act is a reflection of her pride; her outburst showcases the natural tendency of one who is driven by false ego. That's the nature of pride. We think we are in control, we think no one else can take control over us, we think we are superior to others. This kind of a superiority complex results in many anxieties, difficulties and challenges in relationships. A large number of people in the world are under stress and anxiety. One of the main reasons for this is pride. When people find that there are others who are doing better than them, they may not be able to cope with it. They can develop a sense of inferiority and lose hope in whatever they try to accomplish in life.

One way to possibly conquer pride is with proper knowledge: knowledge that we are insignificant, that we are actually a fractional part of the supreme. When we receive this knowledge from a bonafide authority and understand it in the right spirit, we begin to see all living beings in the same way. We understand that although we are insignificant in comparison to the Supreme Lord, we can still make a significant contribution to others in the world and that nobody's contribution is valueless. As a result, the feeling and tendency to compete, conquer and establish one's superiority will be vanquished.

The word 'humility' comes from the word humus which means soil. When the soil is fertile, that is, rich in humility, and if the seeds of service are sown in it, we are able to dovetail our desires and consciousness in such a way that we can do wonders in this world through our significant contributions.

Further, to cultivate humility, the practice of renunciation is important. It's the art of letting go; it quells the mushrooming of pride and also leads to contentment.

Let's discuss the four types of renunciation and the positive outcome they can lead to.

1. Renouncing pride makes one pleasant

When one is proud, the mind is constantly self-aggrandizing. As a result, they are agitated and always look for the company of people who can pander to their vanity. They are not open to being challenged and, if challenged, unable to come to terms with being challenged, they try to absolve themselves, and instead point fingers at others in an attempt to shift blame. Likewise, they are not receptive to feedback and even when constructive feedback is provided, they get defensive. In such a state of mind, one can be perceived as being toxic. When pride is renounced and a person is humble, they are more collaborative, more humane in dealing with people, and as a result, people find them pleasant.

2. Renouncing anger makes one regret-free

As they say, anger is one letter short of danger. Anger is a negative feeling state that is typically associated with hostile thoughts, physiological arousal and maladaptive behaviours. It usually develops in response to the unwanted actions of another person who is perceived to be disrespectful, demeaning, threatening or neglectful. Excessive anger can not just lead to physical but mental health issues as well. Besides these, psychologically, when people calm down after an emotional outburst, they recognize that it was a momentary spike in passion and often regret their actions—verbal or physical. When one is composed and renounces anger, they are in control of such provocative situations and remain free of regret.

3. Renouncing lust makes one wealthy

According to the Chaitanya Charitamrita, 'The desire to satisfy one's own senses is called lust, while the desire to satisfy the senses of Krishna is called prema, love of God.' Further, a verse in the Srimad Bhagavatam describes lust as follows: 'One who accepts material sense objects as desirable certainly becomes attached to them. From such attachment lust arises, and this lust creates quarrel among people.'

Lust is the perverted reflection of the love of God which is natural for every living entity. When a living entity comes in contact with the material creation, his eternal love for Kriñhna is transformed into lust, in association with the mode of passion. Or, in other words, the love of God is transformed into lust. When lust is unsatisfied it turns into wrath; there is always a feeling of inadequacy and the mind craves more. In such a state, one feels that they don't own as much and there is a quest for more and more accumulation of material wealth. When lust is renounced, the inadequacy vanishes, one is grateful for what they already have and feels wealthier.

4. Renouncing greed makes one happy

It is wisely said: 'God has provided for everyone's need, but not for everyone's greed.' An angry man can be pacified when he vents his anger by chastising someone, a thirsty man can be satisfied by drinking some water, a hungry man can be satisfied by having some food. But a greedy person can never be satisfied with anything, no matter how much they accumulate. Due to their passionate mode, people go on increasing their material belongings, thinking that this way they have greater control. But by increasing their material belongings they end up becoming their slaves and get entangled in them. Paradoxically, while they accumulate more and more, the greed makes them think of only what they lack, and they crave even more things. In such a state of mind, they are deprived of satisfaction. However, when greed is renounced, there is contentment which leads to happiness.

FIVE

The Quest for Easy Money

Human Quality: Envy

'One more week pending,' Deepak muttered, looking at the daily sheet calendar on the wall of his compact two-BHK apartment in Ranchi.

Deepak, an engineering graduate, had been unemployed for six months. Following his graduation, his father had promised him pocket money for six months, after which it was up to him to find a job and earn a living. He realized that he was just a week away from completing six months and that he would no longer receive any pocket money for his expenses. He decided to focus and put in more effort into finding a good job.

That evening, enroute to a nearby park for a stroll, he took notice of a medical clinic for the first time. The signboard outside got him curious. It read, 'GET TREATMENT FOR Rs 100. IF NOT CURED GET BACK Rs 1000.'

Deepak sensed an easy and quick opportunity to make Rs 1000 right away; it would solve the pocket-money problem for another month, at least. Deviating from his route, he walked into the clinic.

Deepak greeted the doctor and the doctor inquired why he was there.

'Doctor, I have lost my sense of taste,' Deepak said.

'Nurse,' the doctor called, 'bring medicine from box no. 22 and put three drops in the patient's mouth.'

'Ugh,' Deepak cried, 'this is kerosene.'

'Congratulations, your sense of taste has been restored,' the doctor cheered.

Just then, Deepak realized his folly.

'Please pay Rs 100 to the compounder,' the doctor announced.

Annoyed, Deepak left the clinic. However, he didn't give up and wanted to return for a better deal the next day. Now, he had thought of a better idea and returned a week later.

'I have lost my memory,' Deepak said. 'I cannot remember anything.'

'Nurse,' the doctor called again. 'Please bring medicine from box no. 22 and put three drops in his mouth.'

'That is kerosene,' Deepak blurted out. 'You had given this to me last time to restore my taste.'

'Congratulations,' said the doctor. 'You have got your memory back.'

'Oh my god!' Deepak realized his folly yet again.

'Please pay Rs 100 to the compounder, thank you,' the doctor wished him well.

Fuming, Deepak walked out of the clinic feeling disgusted. He despised the fact that he hadn't thought his plan through and had fallen into the doctor's trap again. As he walked out of the clinic, he felt a pat on his shoulder. It was his friend Lokesh, from college.

'How are you, Deepak? What brings you here to this doctor?'

'Hey Lokesh, what's up, man? Good to see you here.'

Deepak tried to skirt the question about his visit to the doctor but on Lokesh's insistence, he had to give in.

'Well, I came here to make a thousand rupees, but ended up losing a hundred actually.'

'Only a hundred?' Lokesh asked with a smirk.

'Yes, of course.'

'Dude, be careful. My brother has lost five hundred rupees already. This doctor is very smart, and you better not play with him.'

'I am smarter than him, don't you worry,' Deepak affirmed.

'Don't envy him. He's known in this town for being mentally agile and tricking people like you. He's got a stellar record, mind you.'

Unable to bear Lokesh's appreciation for the doctor, Deepak shunned the warning and challenged himself to make his next visit successful.

He took two weeks to devise a plan. This time, he decided not to open his mouth until the prize money landed in his hands. With that resolve, he walked into the doctor's clinic.

'Please tell me, how can I help?' the doctor asked with a smile.

'My eyesight has become weak', Deepak announced with his eyes half closed. 'I am unable to see at all.'

'Well, I don't have a cure for this,' the doctor admitted. 'So, here is your Rs 1000.'

Thrilled, Deepak opened his eyes and stared at the note.

'But,' Deepak exclaimed, 'this is not Rs 1000 but Rs 100!'

'Congratulations, Deepak,' the doctor wished him for the third time now, 'your eyesight has been restored.'

Deepak banged his head on the doctor's table as he returned the currency note to the doctor.

'Please pay Rs 100 to the compounder,' the doctor informed him yet again with a wider smile this time around.

In the Bhagavad Gita (16.4), it is said:

> *dambho darpo 'bhimānaś ca*
> *krodhaḥ pāruṣyam eva ca*
> *ajñānaṁ cābhijātasya*
> *pārtha sampadam āsurīm*

The root cause of finding fault is envy. To start with, let us understand the difference between envy and jealousy.

Envy is when we want what someone else has, but jealousy is when we are worried that someone is trying to take what we have. Jealousy and envy both involve a feeling of desire for what another person has, but jealousy is usually thought to be more negative as it often involves resentment towards the other person. Envy is also a negative feeling—a mix of admiration and discontent—but the word doesn't usually imply hostility. Envy manifests in an immature mind when one sees others succeed.

The following points can be kept in mind as we strive to tackle envy:

- Envy backfires.
- The passive feeling of envy, if not eliminated in the beginning, can turn into action, causing damage to self and others.

- When two people desire the same thing and only one person gets it, the one who doesn't often becomes envious. That is due to the scarcity in this world, and more accurately, the mentality of scarcity of the people here. One needs to bring a mentality of abundance, not scarcity, and have no reason to be envious by cultivating genuine appreciation for people as they are, to address envy in a phased manner.

- Being satisfied with what we have been blessed with is fundamental and can be a good start to addressing not just envy but also lust, anger, greed—the three gates to hell.

- Envy is an indirect glorification of others. If the heart has appreciation for others, why not be direct about it?

SIX

A Tale of Two Brothers

Human Quality: Compassion

In the picturesque town of Kollengode in Kerala lived two brothers, Vikram and Vinay. In the prime of their youth, the brothers lived with their parents in their ancestral property, a large mansion housing over ten rooms and a garden at the back. Kollengode is a site of spotless beauty—the roads are nestled between verdant paddy fields with a mountainous backdrop and the town is surrounded by the Nelliyampathy hills on one side and an expanse of fertile paddy fields on the other. The Gayathri River, a tributary of Bharathpuzha, winds its way through the town. The place is known for its rural setting and, with many festivals organized between December and January, it's a spectacle during the winter season. Located close to Palakkad, Kollengode is home to the Kachamkurissi temple dedicated to Lord Vishnu.

Vikram and Vinay were expert blacksmiths but they also took an interest in farming. Their father had passed away a few months after he turned seventy, and the time had come to divide the farming land between the two of them equally.

The elder sibling, Vikram, was married and had two children while the younger one, Vinay, chose to remain unmarried.

As the land-division exercise drew closure on legal grounds, Vinay thought to himself, 'It's not fair that we have equal land. My brother has two children to feed and I have none. He should have the potential to generate more income than I do.' So, that night, Vinay took a large bag of rice from his barn and left it in his brother's ba. Feeling contented, he returned home. He was now at peace.

The same night, Vikram thought, 'It's not fair that we both have equal land. In my old age my wife and I will have our children to take care of us while my brother will have no one. He should have more grain to sell so that he can provide for himself in his old age.' Therefore, Vikram also secretly left a bag of rice in his brother's barn. The brothers felt happy.

The next morning, they were confused and pleasantly surprised to see that number of rice bags in their respective barns were the same.

They thought to themselves, 'Tonight, I will be sure to take more rice to my brother's farm.'

At different times that night, both gathered a greater quantity of rice from their barn and delivered it to the other's barn in the dark.

The same sequence of events followed: The brothers were puzzled to see that quantity of rice in their barns remained unchanged yet again. Fretful, the brothers thought to themselves, 'This is just impossible! How can this happen? Tonight, I will start early, as soon as it gets dark and I will make absolutely no mistake. I will make sure that the grain is delivered right.'

The third night was lit by a full moon. More determined than ever, each one of them gathered large bags of rice from their respective barns, loaded them on to a cart and slowly hauled it over the hill to other's barn.

At the top of the hill, under the light of the full moon, the brothers noticed a figure in the distance and wondered, 'Who could it be?'

As they looked closer, they recognized each other and noticed the load that was being pulled behind. They realized what had been happening over the last three days. Without saying a word, their hearts filled with love for each other and they embraced each other warmly.

It is very important that we love and respect our family. In today's age of social media, we live more in the virtual world and forget people in the real world. Real happiness is in giving rather than in taking.

In the *Srimad Bhagavatam* (10.22.35), it is said:

etāvaj janma-sāphalyaṁ
dehinām iha dehiṣu
prāṇair arthair dhiyā vācā
śreya-ācaraṇaṁ sadā

It is the duty of every living being to perform welfare activities for the benefit of others with his life, wealth, intelligence and words.

The body is like a computer and the mind is the hard disk. When the mind gets affected by the virus, the hard disk gets corrupted. For the hard disk to function, we need to apply an anti-virus software. Right now, our minds are overwhelmed with greed, pride, lust, anger, envy and illusion.

A manual like the Bhagavad Gita can guide us in accessing this anti-virus software. The Bhagavad Gita is a practical book that helps in clearing various viral *anarthas* (unwanted things) for the whole system of body, mind, intelligence and soul to function at its maximum efficiency.

For a tadpole can't perceive how a frog is able to live outside water. Yet, it isn't aware that it too shall be there once its transformation begins. Likewise, all of us are afraid of change. We try to project what could occur in the future and build various kinds of preconceived impediments in kick-starting our transformation into better versions of ourselves.

What is happiness? Happiness is a state of being. It is not a physical possession or social prestige.

Let's do an experiment.

Can you name the last five Nobel Prize winners?

Or the country which won the most medals at the last Olympics?

I am sure the answer does not come to mind right away. It's understandable because we hardly store information that is not relevant to our day-to-day life, unless we are preparing for competitive exams.

However, if I ask you to name two friends who helped you to get through difficult days, or three teachers who taught you the most valuable lessons, or five people who inspired you to pursue your dreams, it is easier to answer. This simple exercise ultimately reveals that the people who really make a difference in our lives are not the ones with the most awards, accolades or achievements. They are the ones who care, who show compassion, who positively impact us and make us happy. Likewise, we can make a difference in others' lives by caring for them and serving them. Thus, the art of real happiness is cultivating gratitude and a service attitude.

Carl Jung, the famous psychologist, said, 'I don't know who God is but I know one thing. If you don't understand God, you will go crazy.'

Statistics on suicides in India is disturbing. The National Crime Records Bureau (NCRB) released the data for 2021, revealing that 1,64,033 claimed their lives due to various reasons in 2021. This implies a whopping 450 recorded deaths by suicide every single day of the year.[*]

You're not your achievements!

Often in today's society, one's worth is measured by their accomplishments in life. Yet, the truth is that you are not your achievements, and the problem arises when you start building your self-worth based on them. Thus, when certain expectations of achievement are not met, people tend to fall into depression easily.

George Harrison, one among the famous four members of The Beatles, was a multi-millionaire by the age of twenty-five. The Beatles were 'worth' 65 million pounds in 1965 when the members were in their twenties.

---

[*] Varnika Srivastava and Deekshith Pinto, 'India witnessed record 1.64 lakh suicides in 2021; career-related suicides on the rise', Business Insider, 8 September 2022, https://www.businessinsider.in/sustainability/news/india-witnessed-record-1-64-lakh-suicides-in-2021-career-related-suicides-on-the-rise/articleshow/94066711.cms.

Can you imagine receiving a million greeting cards piled up in seven trucks at your doorstep on your birthday? That was the fame George Harrison enjoyed. After a performance, the Beatles arrived at a hotel in Seattle and the towel with which George once wiped his sweat was cut into pieces and sold by the hotel owner for millions of dollars.

The same George Harrison writes in his autobiography that towards the late 1960s he stopped smiling because there was so much intense pressure, internal conflicts and expectations that made the four of them like caged animals. Then he left for India, met with the saints there and said, 'If I could travel the length and breadth of India like a wandering mendicant, I would be willing to give away all my wealth in order to do that.'

This was the realization of the Beatles' guitarist after attaining unimaginable fame. This is proof that achievements can't provide true fulfilment.

True happiness lies in selflessly giving our love to others through acts of service without any ulterior motives. In giving, we receive. Such a love, when given, is received by us in the form of complete satisfaction with ourselves and it fills our hearts with infinite happiness.

SEVEN

Respect, a Lifesaver

Human Quality: Being Personable

In the bustling suburb of Dombivli on the outskirts of Mumbai lived Ajay with his wife and mother. Newly married, he lived in a compact apartment in a housing society. Ajay was raised by his single mother in a lower middle-class set-up; he had lost his father at a very young age. His mother had worked extremely hard day and night to make ends meet for the family. Eventually, after schooling, he pursued a mechanical engineering skill development programme at the Industrial Training Institute (ITI) and then was employed as a technician at a freezer plant in Thane.

Having come up the hard way, Ajay valued every penny he earned. He was grateful to his mother for having raised him to the best of her abilities despite all the hardships she had had to go through. This gratitude influenced his behaviour with others. A soft-spoken person, he showed kindness, compassion and respect to people at all times.

It was a hot and humid evening in the month of June and just as Ajay was about to take a short break, he was told about a technical fault in one of the freezer units.

Along with a team of fellow technicians, Ajay rushed to the deep-freeze unit and got to work. The fault was more serious than he expected. Although he was supported by a few others, they left as it got darker and it became a one-man show. The repair work went on way beyond time. So much so that the security in-charge locked the whole unit, and Ajay was trapped inside the freezer plant. He had taken the necessary precautions, but he couldn't survive with that for the whole night. Mobile phones were not allowed inside the freezer unit, so he had no other medium of communication.

He had almost given up hope and began to wonder whether he was counting his last few moments of his life. Tears began to roll down his eyes as he thought of his ageing mother and loving wife. Just as he was about to give up hope, suddenly the door opened and then there was somebody shining a torchlight in Ajay's direction.

'Help, help', Ajay shouted.

The security guard rushed towards Ajay and picked him up. He could have otherwise frozen to death overnight.

As Ajay got out, he held the guard's hands firmly and thanked him wholeheartedly, 'If you had not come searching for me, I would have frozen to death.'

The security guard smiled back.

Ajay grabbed a glass of water and composed himself. Then, he asked the security guard, 'But, how did you find me? How did you know that I was trapped inside?'

The security guard smiled at Ajay and said, 'Sir, there are more than fifty people who work in this unit. Everyday they come to work but you, my dear friend, are the only person who greets me in the morning with a smile on your face. While going back every evening, you are the only person who again looks at me, smiles at me and says goodbye.'

Feeling lighter, Ajay smiled and said, 'OK . . . so?'

'Because you offer me such love, such respect everyday,' the security guard continued, 'I keep note of when you come and when you go, but today, I never saw you leave at your usual time. So, I went looking for you all around the factory.'

Ajay heaved a sigh of relief and hugged the man tight.

'Yes, sir. I was worried and I am glad that I found you here finally. I thank God for giving me the intelligence to come search for you and eventually rescue you.'

Ajay looked up to thank God, put his hands around the man's shoulder and walked out with his heart overflowing with gratitude.

In the *Chaitanya Charitamrita* (Adi 8.55), it is mentioned:

suśīla, sahiṣṇu, śānta, vadānya, gambhīra
madhura-vacana, madhura-ceṣṭā, mahā-dhīra
sabāra sammāna-kartā, karena sabāra hita
kauṭilya-mātsarya-hiṁsā nā jāne tāṅra cita

Various good qualities like tolerance, respect, self-control, kindness and politeness are all inherent ornaments of great souls. A distinct quality of great personalities is that they offer respect to others.

An eye-opener from this story is how we often live life taking situations and people for granted. We do not realize that a small gesture like offering a smile, good wishes or respect to others can go a long way in positively impacting them; it can even become a lifesaver.

Here, this technician in the ice factory touched the security guard's heart with a simple gesture, wishing him good morning and goodbye every day. In terms of time, this could have hardly taken a minute or two daily, however, the warmth, good intent and consistency of this gesture won his heart. It may have come across as insignificant but when the time came, this apparently insignificant gesture became the cause of a significant rescue operation that saved Ajay's life.

A life led on the principles of compassion, humility and respect makes one personable. Such people are aware of their influence and are careful in choosing their words during conversations. This doesn't come from a need to impress someone; they genuinely care for others, they want to be compassionate and not be hurtful to others.

In the Ramayana, Lord Ram glorifies Hanumanji's speech as *vakya kusala*, an expert's speech.

Some characteristics of vakya kusala are:

- **It shows sufficient time studying under exalted teachers**

  At the core of one's personality is education; knowledge acquired provides the ability to discriminate between good and bad. Learned people are called so not just for the knowledge they possess but also for their ability to apply it with wisdom. It's very important to recognize that the quality of education is not just a function of the curiosity of the student but also how elevated the teacher is. Exalted teachers have the ability to inspire as well as lead by example. When one studies under such teachers their personality is molded by them, and they acquire all the good qualities automatically.

- **The quality of speech reflects their education**
  When one's personality is moulded by studying under exalted teachers, they are balanced in their views and their communication skills become refined. They are aware of the impact of their speech and are circumspect in modulating the tone and tenor of their speech. They are honest but not hurtful. They genuinely share their knowledge without being boastful. They give feedback in a constructive way, with examples, without being condescending or with an intent to find fault.

- **The speech is eloquent, succinct and unambitious**
  Such people have clarity in thought which drives eloquence in speech. They arrive well prepared for conversations, ensure that they have done their due diligence with respect to gathering information and points for the discussion and present their inputs succinctly without beating around the bush. Their conversations or exchanges are carried out with the motive to serve others and not to succeed or overtly impress people. They constantly look for ways to add value, enhance situations and make life better for all people involved.

- **The speed and volume of the speech are consistent from start to finish**

  Although they have clarity of thought and preparation in place, they are neither tempted to speak nor in a rush to present their views. They actively listen to the views of others and possess a learning mindset. Because they maintain equipoise and their mind is still, their speech is both cogent and coherent. They don't raise their tempo to convince people or to leave a lasting impact or to oppose someone with a different view. They only want to explore ways to serve people without expecting appreciation or any favour in return.

- **The speech is holistic**

  Most often, people want to impress others and are very conscious of how they are perceived and adopt various tangential methods to catch the attention of people. For the best speakers, the sole focus is on the WHY, WHAT and HOW of the speech. WHY defines purpose, WHAT covers the content of course and HOW communicates the intent of speech. People tend to typically focus on the WHAT as they prepare for a speech, gathering data, stories and context. However, the WHY and HOW aspects are very important to strike an emotional chord with the audience. WHY lays down the foundation of the speech, it posits its relevance, presents the overarching theme and looks at the big picture. The HOW, on the other hand, communicates the intent of the speech and this is largely reflected in the tone and tenor of the speech.

How one presents oneself showcases the drive behind the speaker's talk, whether it is a constructive presentation or one meant to provoke, polarize or set a false narrative. The HOW aspect goes a long way in building an emotional connect with the speech's audience. This, combined with WHY, forges a sustained connection and commitment to the idea. The vakya kusalas like Hanumanji master the art of speech and impact listeners positively with a focus on the WHAT, HOW and WHY aspects.

EIGHT

Extinguishing Anger

Human Quality: Equipoise

A saintly person was on a riverbank along with his disciples. As they were taking a bath, they heard loud, angry shouts from a distance.

The saintly person turned to his disciples and said, 'Why do you think these people are shouting so angrily at each other?'

One disciple said, 'Because they are agitated.'

Another disciple said, 'They are unable to control their anger.'

A third said, 'The anger has totally overwhelmed and overpowered them.'

A fourth said, 'They are puppets in the hands of anger.'

'Still,' the saintly person responded, 'why should they shout at each other when they are practically next to each other?'

The disciples looked at each other and realized that none of them had a suitable response to that.

'Do you want to take a minute?' the saint asked gently.

Even after a minute, there wasn't anything substantive from the disciples' side.

'When two people are angry with each other,' the saint affirmed, 'the cause of that anger is because their hearts become distant from each other and when the hearts of two people become distant, they try to cover that distance by shouting.'

The disciples felt awakened by the depth of thought in the saint's words.

'When somebody is very far,' the saint continued, 'you can only address them by shouting. So, although physically they are next to each other, their hearts have become so distant that they have no choice but to shout in order to communicate and make sure the message reaches the other person.'

The disciples folded their palms in admiration and thanked him for sharing this wisdom.

'Not just this,' the saint added, 'in contrast, when two people have a healthy relationship, good understanding and genuine love for each other, that camaraderie, affection and love makes them feel closer to each other. Sometimes they don't even have to talk, they just trust each other so well.'

The students learnt a good lesson that day.

In the Bhagavad Gita (16.21), it is said:

tri-vidham narakasyedam
dvāram nāśanam ātmanaḥ
kāmaḥ krodhas tathā lobhas
tasmād etat trayam tyajet

Shri Krishna says that the three gates that lead to hell are greed, lust and anger. So, we must be extremely careful of the influence of these three as they have the potential to destroy our intelligence and capability to discriminate between good and bad.

Anger is usually generated from contact with the three modes of material nature—goodness, ignorance and especially passion. It is also described in the Gita that anger comes from unfulfilled desire. When a desire for sense pleasure is not fulfilled, we become angry. We also become angry when we try to control that which is beyond our control—the behaviour of another person or a situation that doesn't go our way.

PRACTICAL TIPS TO CONTROL ANGER

Hold your breath, try to count from one to thirty to begin with and then chant God's holy names. The names of Shri Krishna are so powerful that they help us overcome all negative emotions we have on our own. When we cannot overcome our emotions, and we surrender to the names, forms, qualities and pastimes of Shri Krishna, He empowers us and through His mercy, we gain the strength to overcome them. By taking the shelter of Krishna, the ripples of agitation in our mind settle and we are able to see the fish as they are.

One more practical suggestion is that whenever we are agitated in life, it is best to stay calm and not react in that moment. Take your time. Stay aloof. You could also isolate yourself if that helps. Think it through in a balanced, unbiased way. Don't think 'I am always right' but be humble enough to see the other person's perspective. When we try doing that, we often see that the fault is ours. So, the need to be angry fades away.

Anger can be controlled at four levels:

1. **PHYSICAL**: This is the most violent form of anger; it can be a nerve racking experience internally and be accompanied by verbal abuse and physical assault externally. This type of anger arises because of rampant rage stemming from the extreme emotions one experiences in provocative situations. One needs to exercise a lot of care in suppressing it. This can be done by curbing one's visual, verbal and physical reactions on time.

2. **EMOTIONAL**: Exercising emotional control is the next step. Here, one looks beyond the physical aspects of anger to recognize the emotional impact of such anger. Here, one truly empathizes by stepping into the other person's shoes and attempting to understand their behaviour and its ramifications. As the famous quote in the New Testament goes, 'Do unto others what you want them to do to you. This is the meaning of the law of Moses and the teaching of the prophets.'

3. **INTELLECTUAL**: At an intellectual level, one can research, study and deeply contemplate on the ill effects of anger. One can learn from relevant sources and convince oneself to curb the reactive instinct. On reading, one finds that the ill effects of anger are not just physical but holistic: physical, mental and emotional. People who control their anger at an intellectual level are driven by logic and they build conviction through a stimulating thought process.

4. **SPIRITUAL**: The highest level at which one can control anger is spiritual. This starts off with the

fundamental understanding that we are not this body but the soul. When we understand our real position as part and parcel of God and our insignificance in the largest scheme of things, we understand how inflated our false ego resulting in anger is. The *Srimad Bhagavatam* describes many persons who conquered lust and were unaffected by anger. Foremost among them is Prahlada Maharaja. At the age of five, Prahlada, a self-realized devotee, had no interest in worldly gain—the opposite of his lustful, atheistic father Hiranyakashipu. In time, the godless Hiranyakashipu began to look upon his saintly son as an enemy and plotted to kill him. Although harassed in various ways by his father, Prahlada never became angry with him. The Lord, however, appeared as Narasimhadeva and killed Hiranyakashipu. Afterwards, He offered a benediction to Prahlada, who, being satisfied in the love of God, asked only that his evil father be liberated from his sins.

One of the biggest problems the world is facing today is dysfunctional families. Anger is an important reason why family bonds break. One heated moment or argument has the potential to ruin relationships. Let us understand the importance of family relationships and then apply the methods to control anger diligently for sustained and positive familial relationships.

It's so important for family members to develop a closer relationship with each other. Skills, formal education and other kinds of knowledge can always be taught in formal educational institutions and other organizations. Anybody anywhere can obtain professional training, but values and the real emotional experience of the heart can only be taught within families. Unfortunately, there is no system that teaches people to take their family values seriously. We find that people are increasingly neglecting the institution of family and family members are spending lesser and lesser time together: in dining together, staying together, talking to each other, praying together, chanting the names of God together and trying to relate with each other with genuine love and affection. Therefore, let us try to invest in our family institutions and reap the benefit of our hearts coming closer and then we can develop more peace and harmony in this institution.

NINE

Power of Positive Communication

Human Quality: Communication

There was a blind man who was seated at the entrance to a skyscraper in New York City. He held a hat by his side along with a sign which read, 'I am blind, please help.'

A few people were throwing some coins in the hat out of compassion and then one young man came by; he was dressed in a suit and seemed to be an investment banker. He saw the sign and put a few coins in the hat. Kind soul that he was, he had a thought, picked up the sign, wrote a few words on the other side, placed it back and walked into the building.

Something changed. Within a few minutes, there was a terrific response to the sign. People were throwing coins left, right and centre into the hat and even the blind man was bewildered.

He asked himself, 'What did this man do, what did he write to cause such a drastic turnaround?'

The day passed by and later that evening, the banker approached the blind man on his way back home. As the banker paced towards the blind man, the latter recognized his footsteps and asked, 'Were you the one who changed the sign this morning after which there was a significant change in people's response?'

'Yes,' the banker smiled. 'I changed the words on your sign and I can see that it has made a difference.'

'Thank you very much,' the blind man responded with folded hands.

'You are most welcome,' the banker tapped him on the shoulder.

Curious, the blind man asked the banker, 'I really want to know, what did you write?'

The banker explained, 'You had the board say—I am blind, please help.'

'That's right,' the blind man affirmed.

'I wrote on the other side of your board—It is a beautiful day, and I can't see it.'

'Oh, I see,' the blind man smiled.

This story is a classic example of how the choice of words which reflects our thought process can make a huge difference. We can see here how people's perception was transformed when the words were changed.

In the first instance when the man proclaimed that he was blind and that he sought help, he was focusing only on himself.

However, later when the sign read that it was a great day and that he couldn't see it, he was indirectly complimenting every passerby, making them realize how fortunate they were. They were able to see, experience, participate in and be part of a beautiful sunny day while he, being blind, was not able to experience the same.

The first message was one of self-pity whereas the second message was one that was infused with gratitude. On reading the second message, people realized how blessed they were and became kind enough to extend help to him.

Communication is a very powerful tool that we can leverage to make a difference to the society at large. It all depends on how we use words to communicate our thoughts and feelings in a way that touches others' hearts

There is a verse in the *Chaitanya Charitamrita* (Madhya 17.133) that goes:

> *nāma cintāmaṇih kṛṣṇaś*
> *caitanya-rasa-vigrahaḥ*
> *pūrṇaḥ śuddho nitya-mukto*
> *'bhinnatvān nāma-nāminoḥ*

The words which carry the all-powerful transcendental meaning is the holy name, which is described as nāma cintāmaṇih, like a touchstone. It is Chaitanya, meaning conscious, rasa-vigrahah meaning all the powers are imbued within the holy name. It is pūrṇaḥ śuddho nitya-mukto meaning it is completely pure, it is liberated and anyone who comes in contact with that transcendental sound also becomes purified. Considering all the above descriptions, it is very important we stay in contact with the transcendental, all-attractive, all-powerful holy names of the Lord. By letting those names communicate to us and by letting ourselves communicate with the Supreme Lord, we let our lives be transformed.

The Lord's holy name is like a fire. Just because a child is about to touch the fire, it doesn't change its natural property.

It indeed burns the finger of the child. Likewise, anything material can never change the supreme potency of the holy names of the Lord.

In Kali, the Lord advents in the form of His holy names. The *yuga* dharma for this age is to perform *sankirtana yagna*, congregational chanting of the Lord's holy names offered as a sacrifice. Thus, it is vital to understand the importance of chanting and how transformative it can be in all our lives.

The first verse of the *sikshastakam*, the only instructions personally left by Shri Chaitanya Mahaprabhu, speaks of the different stages experienced in chanting the Lord's holy names. The fire of sankirtana yagna is compared to the seven tongues of a flame.

1. *Ceto darpana marjanam*—Cleansing of the dust in the mirror

   Consciousness is like a mirror. The soul sees itself reflecting through this mirror. But what if the mirror is covered with thick layers of dust? This dust is referred to in Bhagavad Gita as *kama* or lust, it signals to the self—I'm the enjoyer, I'm the controller. Originally, however, the soul's nature is to be a servant of the Lord. The first tongue of sankirtana yagna cleanses the consciousness of all the accumulated dust carried through innumerable lifetimes.

   We all possess the desire to serve. But we're trapped within the jail of misery. The bars that hold us back distort our path to servitude. These bars keep us diverted towards sensory pleasures. The free world on the other side of the bars is free from the control of senses. The attempts to enjoy more and more and seeking pleasure will get us stuck in a cycle of birth and death.

2. *Bhava mahā dāvāgni nirvāpanam*—Extinguishing the forest fire

The material existence is referred to as forest fire here, and the Lord's holy names have the potency to extinguish this wildfire. Why exactly is material existence compared to a forest fire? Nobody can figure out how a blazing fire in a forest starts, but when it does it devastates an entire ecosystem. If we assume we are not in the middle of a forest fire (material misery) then it is purely because of misunderstanding.

This material creation came into being because of our desires/*ichā*. Free will, when misused, is the beginning of material existence as the soul is trying to create desires independent of the Supreme Lord. The *Jīva* or being may ignite the fire, but he can't put out the fire. That help needs to come from spiritual guides and Krishna. Therefore, the *harinām sankirtan* (the chanting of the holy names) coming from the discipline rains on the top of the fire and extinguishes every burning material desire.

3. *Śreyah kairava candrikā vitaranam*—Chanting is the moon that spreads the white lotus of good fortune for all

Sreyah refers to auspiciousness, kairava to white lotus and candrikā to a moon. After extinguishing the forest fire, the harinām sankirtan acts as moonlight to cool the heat waves of material existence that are still burning us. The moonlight purifies our lustful desires and blossoms the consciousness with real, genuine welfare of the soul.

However, the taste for harinām or *harikatha* isn't instantly developed. Initially, one may find it exceedingly difficult to even chant one round. But later, as one progresses, the unwanted desires fade away and consciousness is slowly purified, and then one can seriously practise his *sadhana*. The same goes for hearing the *Srimad Bhagavatam* and other such pastimes of the Lord. In the beginning, as soon as the speaker gets to reading the purport of Srila Prabhupada, Nidra Devi manifests herself in their faces. Yet, this process of hearing has the power to penetrate through the layers of material reality and touches our souls with transcendental vibrations.

4. *Vidya Vadhu Jivanam*—Knowledge
    Vidya, knowledge is compared to vadhu, a newly married bride. Just as a husband gives shelter to a wife, the harinām sankirtan gives shelter and brings life to *jivanam*, living beings. In the association of harinām, the transcendental knowledge gets fructified just as a husband and wife cooperate to execute their duties. Pure, unalloyed devotional service is the total of all knowledge. And this knowledge is realized only when the Lord's names are sung and the Lord is served with love. That is the power of the holy name. It makes one develop an attachment to Krishna, just as a wife is attached to her husband.

5. *Anandam buddhih vardhanam*—Ocean of bliss
    Harinām sankirtan expands us to the ocean of bliss. Who doesn't like to experience bliss? We have seen different stages of bhakti till *asakht* (attachment). At this stage, the anchor of material life shifts and the ship goes into the ocean and it starts experiencing what is known as

bhava where spontaneous attachment towards Krishna is expressed, and that is what Lord Chaitanya Mahaprabhu mercifully appeared in the age of Kali to demonstrate and through his pastimes.

The Hare Krishna Mahamantra can create a revolutionary churning within our consciousness and help us experience submersion into this ocean of bliss that Mahaprabhu offered. Liberation or *mukti* is nothing compared to this bliss. All of us are aspiring to free ourselves from issues, but this bliss takes us beyond all problem-solving techniques. In other words, this *anandam* doesn't care for a problem-free life.

6. *Pratipadam purna amritam*—Nectar

    The harinām sankirtan helps us taste the nectar or *amrit* with every step we take towards the Lord by chanting His holy names. Amrit also means immortality, which is essential to acquire because the soul is inherently eternal and is always united with God in his service. This nectar of Krishna *prema* is what we're looking for in every moment of our lives. These last two stages refer to the purest form of love—Krishna prema.

7. *Sarvātma snapanam*—Pure love

    The ultimate goal of human life is to achieve pure love for God. Sarvatma indicates that our consciousness is completely submerged in the ocean of unalloyed, pure love for Krishna. And this is attained through the serious practice of harinām sankirtan. When a soul is submerged in love for Krishna, Krishna too reciprocates and he too sinks in an ocean of love for his devotee. This way, both soak in an infinite amount of ecstasy.

We all have a little bit of faith somewhere in our hearts. We can start with that and slowly, from *sradhha* (devotion), we can attain the pure love of Krishna. At this stage, the ray of devotional faith will emerge from us. The holy name pierces beyond all layers of this material universe and opens our hearts to the spiritual world of *Goloka Vrindavan*.

The final words *param vijayate* signify how successfully the harinām has burnt all material desires from our heart and has gained victory in us ultimately desiring nothing but the pure love of God.

TEN

Overcoming Hurdles

Human Quality: Controlling the Mind

It was a pleasant February morning in Pune. Known to be a knowledge capital, with its proximity to Mumbai, the city became a manufacturing hub in the latter half of the twentieth century. In the twenty-first century, the city has become a centre for many software companies, both Indian and global.

Monday arrived and it was buzzing at Talawade IT Park, home to many software companies. Employees had started to arrive to kickstart the work week. The IT Park was home to more than twenty companies and seated more than 5000 employees.

At one such company, there was a commotion at the entrance to the office. Employees stood at the entrance and were seen discussing among themselves. There was a huge board put up at the entrance that read, 'The one who hindered your growth in this company is no longer with us. We invite you to join the funeral in the room beside the cafeteria.'

This message confused everyone who read it. While on the one hand, they felt sad for the death, on the other they were equally curious to know who the person was. There was also a third feeling: happiness that no one would impede their growth and development. A sense of relief was also creeping in. Monday blues vanished into thin air, and the cafeteria area was bustling with energy. Never before had the cafeteria been so lively at half past ten in the morning. The security agents were ordered to control the movement of the crowd and keep it more streamlined.

Suraj, an engineering director and a veteran in the organization with a tenure spanning twelve years, entered the scene. He was a known face in the company and was quite popular among the engineers for his friendly nature.

'Guys, what's going on here?' he asked in surprise.

'Welcome, Suraj,' said a smiling Varsha who worked in his team as senior software engineer. 'We are trying to figure it out too.'

'Never have I seen such a scene in my twelve years here.'

'Totally! I agree,' said Shriram, the software architect who had joined the company a week before Suraj.

'HR typically organizes Rangoli competitions,' added Varsha with a smirk, 'but what is this? And who has done this? That too on a Monday morning!'

The exchange went on for a while and Suraj observed that the reactions of people changed as they approached the coffin.

Intrigued, Suraj wanted to take a look inside the coffin. He quickly made his way to it.

As he looked in, he was confused and his eyes lit up. There was a mirror inside the coffin. People who looked into the coffin saw their own image.

There was also a sign next to the mirror that said, 'There is only one person who is capable of setting limits to your growth, and that is you.'

It's all in the mind, isn't it? You are the only person who can revolutionize your life. You are the only person who can influence your happiness, your sadness and your overall frame of mind. You are the only person who can help yourself. Your life does not change when your boss changes, when your friends change, when your partner changes, when your company changes. Your life changes when you change, when you go beyond your limiting beliefs and when you realize that you are the only one responsible for your life. The most important relationship you can have is the one which you have with your own self. Therefore let us examine ourselves, watch ourselves and not be afraid of difficulties, impossibilities and losses. Let us understand that we have to conquer our false ego, build ourselves and face realities with a controlled mind. It is indeed all in the mind!

In the *Srimad Bhagavatam* (7.8.12), it is said:

> *yas tvayā manda-bhāgyokto*
> *mad-anyo jagad-īśvaraḥ*
> *kvāsau yadi sa sarvatra*
> *kasmāt stambhe na dṛśyate*

The great demon King Hiranyakashipu was under the influence of his false ego. The false ego cannot be destroyed in the day or at night, outside or inside. It cannot be destroyed by any kind of weapons, or by persons living or dead. Therefore it can only be dissolved when each one of us takes responsibility to transform and realize our real ego identity as a facilitator, servant, servant leader and so, with the help of others who are more advanced, talented and more knowledgeable than us, we can make that difference in our lives. You can take a horse to water, but you cannot make it drink. Therefore ultimately you have to take responsibility to begin the journey to change. Let's transform our life from selfish to selfless. From being a controller, proprietor and enjoyer to becoming a facilitator and a servant leader, to becoming an honourable servant in the mission of the Lord and his divine associates.

Let's discuss the mind. The mind can work in mysterious ways, hence decoding it is both intriguing and important. Our mind is a subtle entity capable of thinking, feeling and willing. It is a combination of cognitive and emotional faculties, including intelligence, consciousness, imagination, perception, thinking, judgement and memory, as well as our feelings and instincts.

All of us are aware of our mind but we may have done little to take complete control of it or take care of the problems related to the mind. Let's analyse this.

HOW THE MIND WORKS

All of us have consciousness and this consciousness leads to our attitude. Our attitude leads to certain perceptions. Perceptions determine our behaviour and this behaviour creates memory which influences thought. And thought, in turn, determines the consciousness, forming a complex cycle which needs to be understood properly.

Let's understand this with an analogy. Say you have a close friend whom you know very well, you understand his behaviour and much more. Suppose one day, someone tells you to beware of this particular friend as he is involved in a scandal, and they warn you to be very careful in dealing with him.

Two days later, the friend visits you. The warning given to you earlier rings in your mind and, just as you meet, that momentarily changes your attitude with your friend. You are not able to behave as you did before because your recent perception of him is that he could be a cheat.

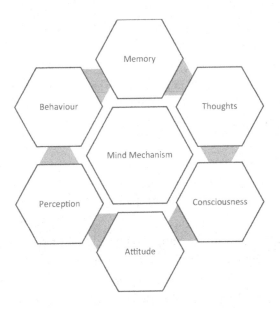

Now, let's say, a few minutes into the conversation, he says he would like to borrow Rs 100 for something he needs to purchase right away. Immediately, you remember what the friend had said, and you are not ready lend him the money because now your perception of this person has changed. This behaviour will in turn determine the kind of memories and thoughts you have for that person.

In this way we are accumulating millions of thoughts every moment, which are deposited in the repository of our mind. Therefore, we need to go through a process of purification of the mind because it accumulates various thoughts at a rate that we cannot deal with.

Let's delve deeper into ideas that can help us in dealing with this barrage of thoughts and help us with control our mind.

When you go to your workplace, you know you are there to work. When you are at a shopping mall, you have decided that you are going there to shop with a list in mind. But if we ask you, why do you go to a temple, what would your answer be? It could be one or more things. It could be because:

- your parents ask you to go there
- your examinations are around the corner
- you are looking for a job change

Everyone goes to the temple with a different purpose, some desires, some frustration, and one performs different types of activities but do you know for what purpose? It is amazing that, throughout one's life, there is one place we regularly go to without knowing the exact reason.

TEMPLE: HOSPITAL FOR THE MIND

A temple can be compared to a hospital. A safe place where treatment is given to the sick mind. The mind is the interface connecting the body and the soul and therefore, we go to the temple to get treated.

Take the case of a surgery we are supposed to undergo. Before we get to understand the treatment procedure we are to go through, we put our trust in the doctor's advice. Likewise, we must first understand the relevance of a temple in this manner. A temple is the clinic where we get a cure for the diseases that plague our soul. It is the hospital where spiritual medicine is distributed. It is also the school where we are educated to regain our mental and spiritual health.

The *Srimad Bhagavatam* (11.13.30) describes a specific way to deal with the mind. In general, you must know which cure you are going to apply, itis a very great deep science and there is no room for speculation.

yāvan nānārtha-dhīḥ puṁso
na nivarteta yuktibhiḥ
jāgarty api svapann ajñaḥ
svapne jāgaraṇaṁ yathā

This line has a simple explanation—if we do not follow the process that is recommended in the scriptures as the ultimate cure and remedy, it will be extremely difficult to cure the mind and purify it of all negative thoughts. There is so much more that can be done to tame the mind.

ELEVEN

Attitude Defines Altitude

Human Quality: Perseverance

Niranjan, a *dhobi*, washerman, by profession, lived in a village in Kalahandi district of Odisha. He earned his daily income thanks to his donkey which helped him carry the clothes for washing to the nearby river. The donkey had been with him for over thirty years and Niranjan had deep gratitude for it and always saw it as a part of his family. The region had experienced severe drought over the past two years and the villagers had to travel more than 4 km to fetch water.

One day, the donkey fell into the dry well located a few metres away from Niranjan's house. It was over 50 feet deep. Hearing the loud cries of the animal, Niranjan rushed out of his house in search of it. In a few minutes, he spotted his companion and felt remorseful. He was at a loss as to what was needed to be done to get it out of the well. He called for his neighbours to help. After a few minutes of discussion, he was informed that the well was going to be covered up, and as the animal was old already, it was not worth retrieving the donkey. Niranjan was not in favour of this advice; he got into a lengthy discussion with the people and tried his best to convince them. However, that was all in vain. He had to give in.

Niranjan said a prayer to God and begged His forgiveness for this act. Reluctantly, he grabbed a shovel and joined his neighbours in the exercise. Together, they all began to shovel dirt into the well. Immediately, the donkey realized what was happening and cried even louder. It felt deep pain and realized death was near. More villagers joined in a few minutes and starting shovelling more dirt into the well. The villagers noticed that the donkey was not crying anymore, rather, it had become quiet. They wondered if the donkey was buried under the dirt. Of all of them, Niranjan was most curious.

He looked down into the well and was astonished at what he saw. As each shovel of dirt hit its back, the donkey was doing something extraordinary. It would shake the dirt off and take a step up. As the villagers continued to shovel dirt on top of the animal, it would shake it off and take a step up. Pretty soon, everyone was amazed as the donkey stepped up over the edge of the well and happily jumped on to the ground to join the rest of the village.

Does this story ring a bell? The cycle of material life shovels dirt on us—all kinds of dirt like defeat, displeasure, disease, the death of loved ones. The lesson to learn from this donkey is the trick of getting out of the well of fear of failure. We should shake the dirt off, brave against all odds and take that step. It's a mindset and we should cultivate one that sees each of our troubles as stepping stones. We can get out of the deepest well just by never giving up, shaking it off and taking a step up.

We start this journey by remembering the four simple rules for happiness:

- Free your heart from hatred, forgive
- Free your mind from worries, most never happen
- Live happily and appreciate what you have
- Give more, expect less from people but more from yourself

Life presents two choices always: we accept reality and deal with it or we surrender to reality, lose hope and become a total nervous wreck. The former is the wiser option to choose.

In the Bhagavad Gita (2.40), Krishna puts it beautifully to Arjuna:

> *nehābhikrama-nāśo 'sti*
> *pratyavāyo na vidyate*
> *sv-alpam apy asya dharmasya*
> *trāyate mahato bhayāt*

'My dear Arjuna, those who are on this path realize that whatever investment we make on the spiritual journey, it is never lost, it is always with us, *sv-alpam apy asya dharmasya trāyate*. And a little progress protects us from the greatest fear. Therefore continue the journey with dedication and put your entire energy and effort in trying your best because we only have control over our effort and our attitude. We do not have control over other people's responses and circumstances.

Likewise, the well-known Zen proverb, 'The obstacle is the path,' is as true today as the day it was coined. We cannot get out of the deep recesses of darkness by feeling sorry for ourselves, nor by spending all our energy in understanding the motives of our wrongdoers. Analysis paralysis has helped nobody and brooding over lost opportunities only hides current opportunities from our sight. Stopping the struggle is not an option. How we deal with it is our choice to make.

Perseverance is the persistence with which we pursue something despite apparent difficulty or perceived delay in achieving success.

The best achievements in life comprise a five-step process. The outline of this process is defined below. We can contemplate on it and pursue life accordingly.

STEP 1: Skill + Activity

Each one of us is blessed with skills based on good karma and desires. This could be writing, mathematical ability, poetry, archery, swimming, etc. The variety and expertise vary from person to person. While skill is one part, engaging in activities that help one hone it and striving for excellence through constant practice can lead to mastery over it.

STEP 2: Activity repeated many times

As they say, practice makes perfect. Even the best batter in the game of cricket hits the nets daily. He/she can't rest on past laurels to remain relevant. Each day is new and they need to approach it that way—they need to practise hard daily if they are to bat to the best of their abilities. As one repeats activities many times, they get tuned to a rhythm and reach a higher level of comfort with skilful performance over time.

STEP 3: Activity performed consistently

With a higher level of comfort with skilfulness, one becomes more consistent in performance. The output may not be the best at first but it gets better with time. As one gets better, it instils confidence within. A higher level of confidence motivates one to strive for perfection and build a never-say-die attitude.

STEP 4: Activity done correctly

As one strives for perfection, one gets closer to doing things accurately. As one continues to engage in such activities with a level of mastery in performance leading to precision in output, one outperforms many of one's peers and starts setting a benchmark for performance in that field.

STEP 5: Superlative achievement

Setting new benchmarks in the field corresponds to superlative achievement. One achieves such levels of excellence only when talent meets opportunity and hard work. Talent is God-given; nurtured with the right attitude and hard work, it can manifest into superlative achievement when the right opportunity manifests itself in the form of favourable external circumstances.

Sustained, long-term success calls not only for perseverance but passion. When they combine, it's called grit. Identifying one's passion is a first step. It should be something one is both good at and is interested in.

Superlative achievement is a combination of:

a. Unusual ability: An unusual ability is the result of tremendous amount of *punya* (good karma) done in one's previous births and it manifests as an exceptional skill that comes naturally with considerably less effort.

b. Exceptional zeal: For this unusual ability to manifest into something tangible and extraordinary, one needs exceptional zeal to pursue it. One needs to tap into the ability and find avenues to exhibit it. This calls for practice, hard work and the capacity to fight against setbacks.

c. Capacity for perseverance: Even the most talented people with exceptional zeal are not spared by the cycles of material life. They go through the ups and downs in life and what determines whether they reach the zenith is their perseverance, the degree to which they can persist, resist pressure and temptations and stay true to their life's mission.

TWELVE

Who Can Escape the Chase?

Human Quality: Service

Once a cow went to the forest to graze. Although it was late in the evening and about to get darker, it wanted to graze on the last few piles of grass for the day. Just then, eyeing the cow as potential prey, a tiger started chasing it. The cow sensed what was happening and, engulfed in fear, began to run. The cow sped through different parts of the forest—some areas were flooded others were covered with dry leaves. The tiger was not ready to give up the chase. After running a long distance, panting and helpless, the cow noticed a pond where it could take shelter for a while and jumped in. The tiger was so desperate to track down its prey that it mindlessly followed the cow straight into the pond.

While it looked like a safe pond at first, it was quicksand. This meant that anyone stuck in it would be dragged deep within gradually over a period of a few hours. Neither the cow nor the tiger realized it. Both were stuck in the quicksand at some distance from each other.

With its prey a stone's throw away but unable to rip its flesh apart, the tiger felt enraged. Every look at the crow added to its anger.

Unable to control its emotions, the tiger warned the cow, 'I am just waiting to attack you and eat you.'

'You are simply helpless,' the cow laughed. 'Stuck in this mud, what can you do?'

'If I get an opportunity, I will finish you off.'

'Only if you get one. . .' the cow smirked.

'It's just a matter of time,' the tiger didn't seem to have lost hope.

'Look,' the cow diverted the topic, 'both of us are drowning in this quicksand but I have a question for you.'

'What's your question?' the tiger asked in a condescending tone.

'Do you have a master?'

'What kind of question is this?' asked the bewildered tiger and then added, 'I am the king of the jungle, I am the master of everyone, how dare you ask whether I have a master or not?'

'Hey,' the cow smiled at the tiger, 'just try to understand. You say you are the king of the jungle but stuck in this mud, what power are you able to exert?'

'How dare you?' the tiger tried to raise itself.

'How much power do you really have? Everything is finished for you in this quicksand. You are going to die in some time.'

'You, insignificant cow,' the tiger retorted, 'don't tell me that I am going to die, you are also going to die.'

'No, I am going to live. Therefore I am asking, do you have a master or not?'

'I cannot understand . . .' the tiger swallowed its words and continued in a lower tone, 'what do you mean? Explain it to me.'

'Well, you do not have a master; I have a master and when he notices that I am missing from the herd after sunset, he will come searching for me.'

'What? Will he come in search of you here?'

'Yes, he will search the length and breadth of the forest and then he will definitely come here. When he sees me, he will take me back, I will be rescued.'

And sure enough, it was sunset. It had begun to get dark and a farmer, the cow's master, started searching for his animal. He shouted the cow's name and the cow responded in a way that the master understood. Within a few minutes, the farmer came to the quicksand and saw that his cow was stuck with its predator only a few metres away. He quickly came closer, rescued the cow and they left the tiger behind. Ultimately the cow was saved while the tiger breathed its last a few minutes from then.

Each one of us in this material world has a choice to make—whether we want to take the shelter of a guru or be a servant of our egoistic mind. The tiger represents the conditioned egoistic mind. The cow represents the surrendered soul. The conditioned mind traps us within the chase of this material world of *adhidaivik* (caused by natural disturbances), *adhibhautik* (caused by other living entities) and *adhyatmik* (caused by the body and mind) miseries and ultimately, we are all trapped in the cycle of repeated birth and death like being stuck in quicksand. But when we take the shelter of a bona fide spiritual master, they can come to us and rescue us.

Therefore, in the *Chaitanya Charitamrita* (Madhya 8.73), it is said:

> *bhavantam evānucaran nirantaraḥ*
> *praśānta-niḥśeṣa-mano-rathāntaraḥ*
> *kadāham aikāntika-nitya-kiṅkaraḥ*
> *praharṣayiṣyāmi sa-nātha-jīvitam*

When the soul has an eternal master such as Krishna, it will eternally find service and shelter at His lotus feet.

On the path of perfection in spiritual life, it's essential to receive guidance from a guru, spiritual master or guide because we can't directly or immediately approach God on our own.

For instance, if you want to meet the president of India, you can't expect to just knock on her door and get an audience. First you need an appointment from her secretary or an introduction through a mutual friend. It is even more so with God. Each one of us has a direct relationship with God because we are His children but realizing this and acting in that direct relationship is possible after we've become pure. A spiritual master selflessly trains and guides us in reviving our relationship with God and is always willing to help in difficult times.

That said, it's very important that we find a genuine master. Let's discuss what the prominent qualities of a spiritual master are. Spiritual masters:

- are well versed in the Vedic scriptures and follow their principles
- identify themselves as a humble servant of God and never claim to be God
- act with full control of their senses and never lose their control

- are impeccable in their moral character
- are fully dedicated to serving God at all times with body, mind and words
- follow a guru who belongs to a genuine line of gurus, a line that extends all the way back to Krishna, the original spiritual master of all

When we strictly follow the guidance of such a spiritual master, our success in spiritual life is guaranteed.

One may ask whether a guru is absolutely necessary. The Vedas (MU 1.2.12) inform us that he is:

> *tad-vijnanartham sa gurum evabhigacchet*
> *samit-panih srotriyam brahma-nistham*

The Vedas enjoin us to seek out a guru; actually, they say to seek out *the* guru, not just *a* guru. The guru is one because he comes from a line of disciples. What Vyasadeva and Krishna taught 5000 years ago is also being taught now. There is no difference between the two instructions.

The founder acharya of ISKCON Society, Srila Prabhupada, mentions in one of his talks: Taking on a guru is not simply a fashion. One who is serious about understanding spiritual life requires a guru. A guru is a question of necessity, for one must be very serious to understand spiritual life, God, proper action and one's relationship with God. When we are very serious about understanding these subjects, we need a guru. We shouldn't go to a guru simply because a guru may be fashionable.[*]

---

[*] A.C. Bhaktivedanta Swami Prabhupada, 'Choosing a Spiritual Master', *The Science of Self-Realization* (Mumbai: Bhaktivedanta Book Trust, 1977).

THIRTEEN

Setting the GPS of Life

Human Quality: Purposefulness

One time, a famous scientist was travelling in a train and the ticket inspector arrived to check for the tickets.

Right away, the inspector recognized the scientist and said, 'Sir, it's such a fortune and honour that you are travelling in this train. We are honoured to serve you.'

'Thank you for your kind words,' the scientist responded.

'Please can you show me your ticket,' the inspector performed his duty.

The scientist touched his shirt pocket and realized the ticket was missing. Getting anxious now, he started searching for his ticket. He searched in his trousers' pockets next and then in his briefcase. He searched frantically, but in vain. He could not believe that the ticket was missing.

'I had purchased it,' he muttered to himself. He apologized to the inspector right away, 'I am sorry, I had purchased the ticket, but I am not able to find it, give me some time.'

'Sir, please don't worry,' the inspector comforted him, 'you are a respectable figure in society and I trust you.'

The scientist smiled back.

'It's OK, it's absolutely fine,' the inspector reiterated and went ahead with his duty to the rest of the compartment.

After a few minutes, as the inspector returned to the seat where the scientist was seated, he saw something strange. He smiled at this world-famous scientist, supposedly the pride of the nation, who was still searching frantically for his ticket.

'Sir,' the inspector tapped the scientist, 'please relax; we have full faith in you, you do not have to search for the ticket so desperately.'

'But sir,' the scientist spoke up.

'Please enjoy the rest of the journey. I am not going to fine you,' the inspector assured him with a smile.

'I know that,' the scientist announced, 'but the problem is that I don't know what my destination station is. I don't know where I am headed.'

Each one of us is together in the journey of life and in that journey, some of us are not aware of what our destination is.

And so, it is described in the *Srimad Bhagavtam* (10.5.25):

> *naikatra priya-saṁvāsaḥ*
> *suhṛdāṁ citra-karmaṇām*
> *oghena vyūhyamānānāṁ*
> *plavānāṁ srotaso yathā*

Just like sticks come together for some time in a flowing river and then dissipate, souls come together for some time, remain together, have various kinds of experiences of happiness and distress, joy and sorrow for a short period of time and then time separates us and this goes on repeatedly.

When you are on the journey, you have to ask the most important question, 'What is my destination?'

This human form of life is a blessing of God and is meant to help us reach the ultimate destination, that which gives eternal pleasure, bliss, knowledge and take us on a platform beyond death, and beyond birth too. That GPS which helps us set our destination is the beautiful book, the Bhagavad Gita. Right through the eighteen chapters, Lord Krishna presents various options of destinations, and at the end of it all, He also gives his recommendation when He says in the Bhagavad Gita (9.34):

man-manā bhava mad-bhakto
mad-yājī mām namaskuru
mām evaiṣyasi satyam te
pratijāne priyo 'si me

'My dear Arjuna, those who are constantly thinking about me, meditating upon me, become my devotee, offer obeisance to me, they come back to me without fail.' Let this highest possible goal be our destination in our human life and our life will surely be successful.

William Shakespeare writes about the phase of a young adult in his famous 'All the world's stage' monologue: 'Then a soldier, / full of strange oaths and bearded like the pard, / Jealous in honour, sudden and quick in quarrel, / seeking the bubble reputation / even in the cannon's mouth.'

This is the psyche of a man who is emerging as an adult, filled with passion to serve a purpose, setting certain goals and grooming himself as a grown-up. He commands respect and instantly protests when his honour is questioned. But this beautiful period of our life where we could use our full potential goes to the gutter when the motivation within is misdirected by external allurements.

The power of media is such that it enamours us through advertisements promising cheap enjoyment and takes away the vitality of our lives. Youth is the most crucial time of our lives. We need to take stock of where we invest our energy and resources, how are we utilizing our God-given intelligence. To be clear in such decision making, we must be diligent in our intent and inspiration.

The three modes of material nature—goodness, passion and ignorance—can create three kinds of inspiration:

- The mode of goodness inspires to maintain
- The mode of passion inspires to create
- The mode of ignorance inspires to destroy

Whereas, in Krishna Consciousness, the basic motto is to inspire every soul in the human form to achieve the ultimate goal of life, which is beyond the above three modes of material nature.

WHY NOW, WHEN WE ARE YOUNG?

Some of us may contradict, 'We agree that we have to cross this material ocean and enter the spiritual world, but what's the hurry? We have got a whole lifetime ahead of us. We can't enjoy it at the age of sixty or seventy. Youth is the time we get to experience all varieties of enjoyment of the senses. Why bother about subjects like spirituality?' But how can you tell who is young and who is old?

WHO IS YOUNG AND WHO IS OLD?

The typical responses are, 'When I cannot walk any longer, then I'll be old.' Or, 'When I cannot properly chew food, then I'll be old.' Well, several youngsters also lose their legs and are unable to walk, and even children's teeth fall away and they can't chew the food properly. From the spiritual perspective, there is only one understanding of youth and old age and that is proximity to death. When one is close to death, he is defined as old and when one is far away from death, he is defined as young.

DEATH IS EQUAL FOR EVERYONE

We must realize that death can devour us at any moment. The recently experienced Covid-19 pandemic is a telling proof. We read so many news stories of people losing their loved ones unexpectedly, and some of them were young people. In the world we live in, people fight for equal rights but death generously provides it. Death transcends boundaries of gender, caste, creed, nationality, race, etc.

Therefore, we must appreciate the fact that we don't have much time in this body. It's important that we utilize and invest time in cultivating love of God as this is the only path that can help us transcend the cycle of birth, death, disease and old age. As souls, we are part and parcel of God. Forgetting this simple fact has led to a snowball effect of utter ignorance and has pushed us to the dualities of material enjoyment and suffering in this temporary world.

Realizing this as early as possible will help us purify our consciousness, replete with contamination arising due to conditioning from several million lifetimes. We can purify our consciousness by serving the purpose God has created us for. Only that shall deliver us from the clutches of illusion.

FOURTEEN

The Vision of Gratitude

Human Quality: Compassion

Seventeen-year-old Anand boarded the Deccan Queen Express at Pune along with his father. It was a cold December morning, and the teenager was eagerly looking forward to the journey. They were travelling to Mumbai for the weekend to attend a family function. Anand's excitement was palpable and it seemed unusual for a teenager. There was a couple sitting right across them who were surprised by the boy's unabashed enthusiasm.

As the train moved out of the station, the joy in Anand knew no bounds. He looked out of the window and shouted looking at the trees, 'Papa, the trees are moving behind us.'

'Yes! That's right,' the father cheered Anand.

The couple seated next to them felt uneasy with his loud cheering for something so normal.

In a few minute's time, as another train passed by in the opposite direction on the parallel track, Anand cried, 'Papa, look there is another train going against us. Wow!'

Again, this loud cry put off the couple yet again.

'Yes, there are two trains,' the father acknowledged his excitement, adding to the couple's displeasure.

'What happened to this boy?' the lady questioned.

'Why is he acting like a child?' the gentleman added.

The father kept quiet, patted the boy and politely told him to speak in a low volume so that he didn't disturb fellow passengers.

After few minutes, as the train approached Lonavala, the scenic beauty prompted the boy to cry out yet again.

'Dad' he called out. 'Just see the clouds! Some are moving behind while some are running with us.'

This unsettled the couple, they found this very strange and the gentleman asked the father, 'Is something wrong with your son?'

'I think so too,' the lady added. 'He looks like an adult, but he is behaving like a child.'

Polite and humble, the father turned to them and said, 'Actually, he was blind from birth and recently, just a week ago, he got his eyesight after a medical treatment.'

This made the couple feel sorry for the boy.

'This is his first experience of a train journey with clear vision,' the father added, full of empathy for Anand.

The couple apologized and wished Anand well.

Sometimes in life, we take things for granted. We don't always realize the value of the gifts we are blessed with. And therefore, it is said, a heart that throbs with gratitude is the most blissful. When we look at others, we should not judge them and recognize that each one of them have their own story. If we remain non-judgemental, then our entire life can be transformed.

In the *Srimad Bhagavatam* (11.14.26), it is said:

yathā yathātmā parimṛjyate 'sau
mat-puṇya-gāthā-śravaṇābhidhānaiḥ
tathā tathā paśyati vastu sūkṣmaṁ
cakṣur yathaivāñjana-samprayuktam

Just like a surgeon performs a surgery to make a person see with his eyes and the patient expresses gratitude to the doctor who has given him that vision, similarly, we need someone to come forward and give us the right spiritual vision. We may have our material eyes, but our spiritual vision is still blinded. With spiritual vision we can appreciate what is reality and what is illusion. When we start looking at this world with the understanding of the world beyond, then our life is filled with an exhilarating joy and bliss because we see the magic, power, and touch of the divine in each and every atom and fraction of this creation.'

As we receive this divine light of spiritual knowledge, it becomes important that we transmit this light, in other words, share this knowledge with others so that they can find meaning in life. For us to be able to do it, we should show compassion.

The divine quality of compassion manifests in four ways in response to focused dedication:

1. Willingness to serve brings empowerment and makes service highly effective

Compassion starts with a service mindset. Since time immemorial, we have been conditioned to material life and have a tendency to enjoy ourselves. As a result, we find it easier to receive than to give. However, real happiness is in giving by cultivating a service attitude. The joy that permeates the heart as we intentionally create a positive impact on someone's life is unparalleled. As we reflect on the difference we create in people's lives, we gather the strength and zeal to do more. This strength and zeal combined makes service highly effective.

2. **Empowerment from the divine realm comes when you gladly offer all your expertise to help others**

   As we make more genuine efforts to serve people, the Supreme Lord empowers us with more strength and zeal to be able to transform the hearts of thousands of people. People often have a thought process that if they give more, they could lose what they have. This could well be true from a static, material standpoint. However, *seva* (service) when spiritualized transcends material limitations. The Supreme Lord, who is the cause of all causes and the source of all sources, empowers the sincere spiritualist with abundance and ensures there is no dearth of ability, strength, capacity or resources for the service to continue.

3. **The divine reciprocates by awarding you increased responsibilities**

   As the Supreme Lord empowers one with more strength and capacity, He adds increased responsibilities for the individual to put it to full use. As they say, with great power comes great responsibility. This can also be construed as a test by the divine to evaluate whether we fall to temptations or continue to engage in a service mindset.

4. **The divine reciprocates selfless, excellent service with
    complicated, difficult duties**

    This may confuse some. Why would the divine reciprocate
    selfless service with difficult and complicated duties? It's
    simple: the sincere spiritualist doesn't think of the self as
    the doer. They know well that they are a mere instrument
    of the will of God. They know that it's the Supreme Lord
    who empowers them to carry out services, whether simple
    or difficult. As the divine presents more difficult duties,
    it's an opportunity for the spiritualist to remember Him
    more often, seek His guidance in prayer and be more
    connected to Him. This just strengthens their spiritual
    bond with the Supreme Lord.

FIFTEEN

Little Boy's Job Appraisal

Human Quality: Self-Development

A little boy went to a drugstore and requested the owner that he be allowed to make a call. When the owner agreed, he climbed on to a carton to reach the landline and dialled a number. The conversation went as follows:

Boy: Ma'am, can you give me the job of cutting your lawn?

Lady (at other end of call): Sorry, but I already have someone to do that job.

Boy: Ma'am, I will do it for half the price you pay the person working on your lawn.

Lady: No, thanks for the offer but I am satisfied with the work of the person employed here.

Boy: Ma'am, I request you one last time. If you give me the job, I will even do additional tasks like sweeping your sidewalk. You will have the prettiest lawn then.

Lady: No, but thank you, young boy.

With a smile on his face, the boy hung up the phone.

The drugstore owner, who was listening all this came to boy looking curious.

'Son,' he said with a smile, 'I liked your attitude and positive spirit and would certainly like to offer a job to you.'

'Thank you, sir, but I can't take it.'

Confused, the owner replied, 'But you were pleading for a job on the call, weren't you?'

'I don't really need a job,' the boy responded with a smile. 'I was just checking on my performance at the place where I work.'

'Sorry, I don't get you,' the owner said, seeking clarity.

'Actually, I work for the lady whom I just spoke to. I wanted to genuinely know whether she was happy with my work and if there are areas I can get better at.'

The drugstore owner became even more pleased with the positive attitude of the little boy and the growth mindset he demonstrated.

In the *Damodar lila* pastime of Lord Krishna, there is a famous verse from the *Srimad Bhagavatam* (10.9.18) which goes:

> *sva-mātuh svinna-gātrāyā*
> *visrasta-kabara-srajah*
> *drstvā pariśramam krsnah*
> *krpayāsīt sva-bandhane*

'Because of Mother Yashoda's hard labour, her whole body became covered with perspiration, and the flowers and comb were falling from her hair. When child Krishna saw His mother thus fatigued, He became merciful to her and agreed to be bound.'

Those who dedicate themselves to self-development demonstrate the following traits:

1. **Harmony in purpose, passion and profession**

    Purpose is the starting point. Purpose defines the 'why' and lays the foundation for our pursuit. It reflects the overarching reason for our pursuit and provides meaning to what we do. Understanding our core purpose is very important. Passion refers to what one has a flair for; what really drives one and what one enjoys doing. As the famous saying goes, 'If you do what you love, you'll never work a day in your life'. People dedicated to self-improvement ensure that their profession is closely linked to their passion. That way, they are self-driven in their profession and, as a result, always pursue excellence and seek to find ways to improve.

2. **Resilience in the midst of adversity**

    In life, encountering challenges or adversity is normal. Its intensity may vary from time to time, but the nature of the material world is such that everyone is put through tough situations. As they say, 'Pain is inevitable but suffering is optional.' How we respond to adversity is key. Those who are pessimistic and with a closed mindset will blame external circumstances while those with a growth mindset and keen on self-development will look for learning and exhibit mental toughness. They display resilience in the face of calamities and ensure they only get stronger after having experienced the calamity. They strive for self-development.

3. **Integrity in character**

    'Doing the right thing when no one is looking' is a common definition of integrity. Integrity is a moral virtue that serves as the foundation of a good character. To clarify, honesty refers to sincerity or truthfulness whereas integrity has a much broader meaning encompassing honesty as well as moral soundness. People with integrity demonstrate harmony in thoughts, words and action. People focused on self-development are true to their conscience and act in line with what is morally right. Such a person periodically takes stock of their behaviour, introspects and find ways to get better with time.

4. **Dedication to service without selfish consideration**
   One reason why people focus on self-development is because they want to be able to serve better. It's not to take pride in their development. As they focus on developing themselves, they build better capability and become better equipped to contribute more effectively. They strive to have a larger impact on society at large. Considering they are focused on self-development, they are dedicated to the service of others as they want to get better always. Dedication is the starting point for it.

5. **Self-confidence in their mission**
   One who is focused on self-development is steadfast in their mission. With a broad-minded worldview and the right intent, they believe in their abilities and are confident that they will achieve the outcome. They don't view feedback as fault finding; they keenly watch out for areas of development, view them as opportunities to learn and consistently get better. With a resolve to get better, they have a high degree of self-confidence in their mission.

6. **Conservative in choosing intimate associates**
   With razor-sharp focus on self-development, they are extremely conscious of, and careful about, whom they

engage with. They are conscious of their acquaintances, their friends, and most importantly, their intimate associates. While external situations demand that they get acquainted with select individuals, they filter out friends and other associates based on the positive impact they have. They look for people they can learn from, those who inspire them, those that they see as confidantes and those who would provide them constructive feedback. They don't want the company of people who could mislead them or create disturbances in their path to self-development.

SIXTEEN

Secret of Pointed Effort

Human Quality: Determination

In the Kutch district in Gujarat lived Ramlal. The village he lived in faced severe drought that year. Summer had just begun and Ramlal was keen to find a source of drinking water. One morning, he began to dig a well near his house. He prayed to God and began the exercise with enthusiasm. He spotted a place just a few yards from his house. He dug up to 20 feet, but no water emerged. And Ramlal began to feel tired, upset and helpless.

Just then, his neighbour came by. He saw what Ramlal was doing and commented, 'Ramlal, you shouldn't dig here.'

'Why not?' Ramlal asked.

'That's not conducive. I will show you where you should.'

He took Ramlal to another spot, 30 feet away. Without asking another question, Ramlal started digging there. He dug up to 30 feet and saw no trace of water. He felt cheated and hopeless now.

He thought of seeking advice from a senior person. He walked into the *tahsildar*'s house and sought help. After a brief conversation, the tahsildar advised him to start digging at a new spot about 50 feet away from the previous spot.

Again, he dug up to 30 feet yet, the result was the same. Absolutely no trace of water.

Dejected, he threw the tools and walked into his house, terribly upset. His father saw sadness writ all over Ramlal's face. He approached Ramlal with a glass of water to quench his thirst on that hot summer morning.

'What happened, my dear son?'

'I dug more than 80 feet and found no trace of water.'

'I am surprised this is the case because as per what I read in the news reports, we should be able to find water at 50 feet.'

Then, after probing further, Ramlal explained what had happened.

'The real issue is not the place,' his father announced.

'What are you saying?' a confused Ramlal questioned.

'Yes, Ramlal,' his father explained. 'So far, you have dug 80 feet across three places based on advice of different people.'

'Yes, that's right.'

'If only you had stuck to digging at one spot and continuously dug beyond 50 feet, you would have found water.'

Ramlal realized his folly.

'Therefore,' his father concluded, 'whenever you try, you should make an effort to go deep and to create and impact.

In the Bhagavad Gita (4.38), it is said:

na hi jñānena sadṛśaṁ
pavitram iha vidyate
tat svayaṁ yoga-saṁsiddhaḥ
kālenātmani vindati

When we have begun the journey to acquire transcendental knowledge, it is not going to be an easy process, we have to keep putting in effort to receive knowledge from deep within our heart. This requires tremendous concentration, focus and a relentless desire to please and serve the Lord and connect with him.

Discipline is very important whenever we take on any assignment, especially when it's arduous and time consuming. Let's discuss this further.

WHAT IS DISCIPLINE?

Discipline is doing the right thing at the right time for the right reason. It can so happen that one does the wrong thing at the right time for the right or wrong reason. Sometimes the time is not always appropriate. Likewise, various permutations and combinations are formed according to the games played by the three modes of material nature. But when a righteous action is performed at the right time for the right reasons, it results in a greater good. Discipline is to bring these three in alignment to propel a higher purpose within, to become an instrument of superior cause. At the battlefield of Kurukshetra, Lord Krishna instructed Arjuna to act on this principle by triggering his sense of duty. If not used at the right time for the right reason, Arjun's years of discipline over his skills of warfare would have gone to ashes.

DISCIPLINE: A REFINING FIRE BY WHICH TALENT BECOMES ABILITY

Everyone is blessed with potential talent. Yet, unless that talent is put through the fire of discipline, their transformation doesn't take place. A lump of coal needs to be put under intense pressure to become a diamond and gold needs to be melted under fire to be made into a valuable ornament. The laws of nature are designed this way. As human beings, this is applicable for us too.

An interesting anecdote from the life of Isaac Newton reveals to us his disciplined efforts to reach his goals. A neighbour of Newton always found him spraying bubbles every morning for eight hours in the hot sun. She thought he was childish and jobless. However, later she came to know he was writing his theories on the laws of physics through such experiments. Thus, although sometimes such acts appear foolish or simple compared to others' extravagant endeavours, consistent effort can bring out the best abilities in man. Newton was highly talented but one of his strengths was that he coupled his talent with a lot of diligent effort. Without that effort of refining fire, the talent cannot become an ability.

DISCIPLINE: DOING WHAT YOU DON'T WANT TO DO SO YOU CAN DO WHAT YOU WANT

When beginning a new task, it is extremely difficult to perform. One may not have honed their skills to perform efficiently, and one may also lack particular behaviours to be proficient at the task. However, one would have entered into that unfamiliar territory with certain goals in mind. The best way to get started is to begin by doing things you wouldn't like to do. Nobody likes studying but good results in exams are earned through consistent effort to learn the subjects. Even Arjun didn't want to fight the battle of Kurukshetra. But he had to do so by following the instructions of the Gita with great tenacity to achieve desired results.

One more personality of note is Arnold Schwarzenegger, the famous Hollywood star, former governor of California and seven-time international bodybuilding champion. He wanted to become a bodybuilder and his father put him into a training regime. Although bitter in the beginning, he could taste the results of the transformation this training brought him. Interestingly, he noted that despite being able to lift only a certain amount of weight during practice, when standing amid millions of spectators during the championship, he lifted more than what he had imagined. This is proof that drastic advancements can be made when we are monitored by the right authorities. As is popularly known, 'No pain, no gain'.

In any practice, spiritual or otherwise, the progress is gradual and ordinary when done alone. Naturally, spiritual discipline requires doing what one doesnt want to do, like waking up early, sitting in place to recite the holy aames of God for two hours, etc., but when accompanied by seekers of the same goal, there are excellent benefits of being motivated and pushing to perform activities out of your comfort zone.

The tendency of a soul conditioned by material life is to take the easy way out. However, the easy way is not the happy way. And good things never come easy. Discipline is doing what you don't want to do so that in future you can do what you have been wanting to do.

SEVENTEEN

Selfishness Is Self-Destructive

Human Quality: Selfishness

Three robbers broke opened a palatial house in central Kannur in northern Kerala. The occupants of the house were on an overseas trip for a week. It was pitch-dark under a new moon that Sunday night. Located at the corner of a residential locality, away from the main road, the street was home to independent houses. In the absence of security guards, the robbers did not have much to worry about. Within an hour, they managed to burgle successfully, piling up the jewels and loose cash into a large bag and rushing out of the scene. They jumped over the walls of the Payyambalam park and gathered at one corner of it, a stone's throw away from the beach.

As they gathered, they started to talk.

'Actually,' began one, adjusting his *lungi*, 'it is not good for us to carry this loot.'

'Yes,' agreed the second, twisting his moustache.

'Let us bury it deep into the forest so that we can take it later,' the third proposed.

They quickly agreed to the plan. They dug up one corner of the park and buried that loot under an ashoka tree.

Like how they were in unison about burying the loot, they all had one more thought in common which they hadn't revealed openly; each wanted to take the loot for himself.

'I am feeling very hungry,' announced the second robber.

'Let me go and get food for all of us and we can eat together,' the third robber suggested.

'Yes,' nodded the first. 'We have had a successful but draining night at work.'

The third robber walked up to a seafood stall by the shore while the other two waited in the park, protecting the loot. As the third walked out, the two in the park began to talk and concluded that they would kill the third robber and split the loot among themselves. However, both of them were also secretly thinking of how they could kill the other. But that was for later; they were focused on killing the third robber for the time being.

As the third robber walked to the food stall, he thought, 'If I am able to poison this food, all of the booty will be mine.'

Just the very thought made him ecstatic. He walked faster now, purchased some food and poisoned it on his way back to the park. He entered the park, approached his partners in crime, and as soon as he placed the food packets on a nearby bench, he met with the unexpected. He was brutally attacked with clubs and fell down unconscious. The two thieves were relieved by the absence of the third. While they were individually plotting to finish off the other, their hunger pang took precedence and having an extra share of food made it even more attractive. If only they knew what the food packets contained.

In the Bhagavad Gita (16.13–14), it is explained:

idam adya mayā labdham
imaṁ prāpsye manoratham
idam astīdam api me
bhaviṣyati punar dhanam
asau mayā hataḥ śatrur
haniṣye cāparān api
īśvaro 'ham ahaṁ bhogī
siddho 'haṁ balavān sukhī

The demonic mentality means that each person thinks, 'I am the superior and I can defeat the others with my power', and in this way the demon is constantly scheming, plotting, calculating how he can expand his influence and destroy the influence of others.

Let's try to transform our heart from the demonic mentality, move on the divine path and make our life successful.

The demonic mentality is characterized by selfishness and such people tend to show the following behaviours. This way, it will be easy for us to identify, stay away from and also ensure that we do not cultivate selfishness.

1. **Lustful**
   The primary motive of those with a demonic mentality is enjoyment of the self. They gratify their senses, pander to their sensory needs (the most dangerous of these being those of the tongue and genitals) and do whatever it takes to enjoy themselves.

EIGHTEEN

Twist in Meditation

Human Quality: Celibacy

In Churthu village in Uttarakhand lived Kedar Sharma, a Sanskrit scholar. He lived with his family in an ancestral property spanning three grounds of land. He came from a lineage of Vedic scholars who were revered in the district. The palatial house that they lived in was so well positioned that from its terrace, one could have a darshan of the *Devprayag sangam*. People from all over the world throng to this sangam where the two heavenly rivers Alakananda and Bhagirathi come together to flow as Ganga thereon. Located over 2500 feet above sea level, Devprayag means godly confluence in Sanskrit.

Despite being married for more than fifteen years, Sharma's wife couldn't beget a child. Sharma consulted various astrologers and performed many pujas to please respective *devatas*, however, begetting a child remained out of reach for the couple. Sharma taught Sanskrit at a well-known *gurukula* and spent time at home studying the Vedic scriptures. Sharma had a superiority complex about his lineage and scholarship and typically looked down on people who lacked education, were menial and belonged to a lower stratum of society.

Just opposite Sharma's house lived Neela, who had been a prostitute since her teenage years. The house she lived in had trees covering the entrance. Orphaned as a child, Neela entered this profession due to trying circumstances that demanded her to make ends meet on her own. Further, an absent father and lack of guidance from elders in the family fuelled this decision. She lived with a friend who worked as a hair stylist at a salon for women.

Although circumstances forced her life to be this way, she had deep admiration for Kedar Sharma. She respected him and always wondered how she could be as well-read, scholarly and *dharmic* as he was. Whenever she would see Sharma pass by, she would fold her hands and say namaste from the entrance gate. On the other hand, Sharma always looked down upon her and never quite reciprocated her respectful behaviour. He felt a deep aversion that such a lowly person was demonstrating such behaviour towards him.

Sharma preferred to be seated at his study table on the terrace in the evenings. With a cool breeze from the riverside, it made the ambience pleasant and was the perfect setting for him to be engaged in the study of scriptures or be deeply absorbed in meditation. While a glance to the north provided a darshan of the holy Ganga River, the southern direction offered a view of Neela's shady house.

Sharma tried best to look north most of the times, but thoughts of Neela and her dressing sense crowded his mind. The dense cover of trees outside her house made for an obstructed view and the lack of transparency made him more curious. While at times he would wonder why she was engaged in such lowly activities, sometimes he was curious about who was entering and leaving her house, where she was headed, etc. Sometimes, during late evenings, he would be engrossed in thinking what she was up to. Swayed by his thoughts, he would peek in her direction, knowing well that nothing was visible. Such thoughts disturbed him during his study and meditation.

One evening, Sharma was returning home from the gurukula. Knowing when he would be on his way back, Neela waited at the entrance of her house to pay her respects to the scholar. Sharma took notice of her and, though in two minds, looked fleetingly in her direction and was indeed drawn to her attractive demeanour. Just then, a lorry entered the street. Unfortunately, the driver lost control of the vehicle, and unable to apply the brakes, he wanted to avoid hitting Sharma and swiftly turned right. The lorry still ran over Sharma at that speed, and as it turned, knocked down Neela as well. Eventually, the vehicle bulldozed into Neela's house. Both Sharma and Neela died on the spot.

A few moments after they passed away, the *Vishnudutas*, agents of Lord Vishnu, came to take the prostitute and the agents of death, *Yamaraja*, came to take away Sharma. This bewildered Sharma.

Right away, he asked the agents of Yama, 'Is there a mistake here?'

'What do you mean?' the agents asked.

'I am such a proficient scholar,' he remarked authoritatively, 'I dedicated my life to studying the scriptures. Now why have the agents of death come to take me?'

'Yes, you were a scholar,' one agent replied, 'but your entire meditation was on the prostitute and the activities of the prostitute.'

The agents added further, 'Whereas she was in that situation due to circumstances she was constantly thinking about how glorious your profession was, how dharmic you were and how fortunate you were to be able to study complex Sanskrit grammar in the scriptures.'

This was a revelation to Sharma.

They concluded, 'In this way, although she was in abominable external circumstances, she positioned herself in good consciousness internally.'

In the *Srimad Bhagavatam* (11.23.42), it is said:

> *nāyaṁ jano me sukha-duḥkha-hetur*
> *na devatātmā graha-karma-kālāḥ*
> *manaḥ paraṁ kāraṇam āmananti*
> *saṁsāra-cakraṁ parivartayed yat*

Many a times, we may think that the cause of our distress are fellow people, the *devatas*, the planets, karma, etc. but the actual cause of distress is our own mind. For one who is unable to control their mind, it becomes their own enemy.

This human form of life has been awarded to us to focus our attention and abilities on what is ultimately the final destination—the spiritual world beyond this material world. Let us use this opportunity to focus all of our mind and all of our attention in controlling our thoughts and desires so that we are ultimately able to meditate on the Supreme Lord and attain him without fail.

One of the greatest celibates we read about in the Vedic Scriptures is Hanuman. As the servant of Lord Ram, he was an epitome of sincere service, one who practised control over his mind and selflessly served the Lord. His great qualities are as vast as the sea. However, for now, let's taste a few drops from them:

Devotion

When Lord Ram's time in Lanka ended and He returned to Ayodhya, the *vanara sena* joined along. At that time, Shri Ram wanted to reward Hanuman. Here goes their exchange:

sneho me paramo rājaṁs tvayi nityaṁ pratiṣṭhitaḥ
bhaktiś ca niyatā vīra bhāvo nānyatra gacchati

When Lord Ram asked Hanuman, 'What do you want in return for the wonderful service you have rendered to me?'

Hanuman spoke thus, 'My dear Lord, let me always have love for you, let me also be affectionate towards you, that is all I want.'

Service

Lord Ram at one point told Hanuman:

Sesasya iha upkaranam
Bhavanu rinrinino vayam

This meant that Lord Ram felt indebted for all the wonderful services Hanuman had performed and would continue to perform.

Hanuman had selflessly carried out innumerable acts of beneficence just as the ones described here, which are the qualities of a true Vaishnava. He is the epitome of pure devotional service. Similarly, in the *Srimad Bhagavatam*, Shri Krishna tells the *gopis* of Vrindavan, 'It is not possible for me to repay the debt. I cannot pay you salary.'

It's the attitude of service and devotion of the devotee that moves even the Supreme Lord to give Himself to the devotee.

Non-Envy

As Hanuman was on his way to Lanka, he had to confront the demoness Surasa. This was a challenge. In spite of Hanuman explaining his mission, Surasa blocked his path and told him that he could pass only through her mouth, as per a boon given to her by Lord Brahma. Hanuman countered by challenging her to open her mouth wide enough to eat him (*bheda* or threat). He started expanding his form and becoming larger, and Surasa also expanded her jaws so she could devour Hanuman; this contest is interpreted as *danda* (punishment). Finally, when Surasa's mouth expanded to a hundred *yojanas*, Hanuman suddenly assumed a tiny form (the size of a thumb) and entered her mouth and left it before she could close it.

The lesson we learn from Hanuman here is that he had no envy. While he had the ability to expand, he also had the large heart to shrink in size. It was not about who between the two was bigger in size. His mission was to serve Lord Ram and he was willing to do anything that served his purpose.

Self-control

After Hanuman entered Lanka assuming the size of a cat, he entered Ravana's inner chambers. He glimpsed Ravana's wives sleeping, they were improperly dressed.

kāmaṁ dṛṣṭvā mayā sarvā viśvastā rāvaṇastriyaḥ
na tu me manasaḥ kiṁ cid vaikṛtyam upapadyate

As soon as he momentarily glanced at them, he realized his position as a celibate, and immediately looked away to continue his search for Mother Sita. This is a lesson on self-control. Even though he was unaffected by lust, he refocused on his mission right away.

Commitment

Hanuman went through multiple trials and tribulations but remained selfless in service and dedicated to the mission. He did all of this simply because he had promised Lord Ram that he would serve Him and help reunite Him with Mother Sita. Hanuman was committed to keeping his promise. When he returned, Lord Ram embraced him.

eṣa sarvasvabhūtas tu pariṣvaṅgo hanūmataḥ
mayā kālam imaṁ prāpya dattas tasya mahātmanaḥ

Lord Ram said, 'My dear Hanuman, I am in exile. I don't have anything to award you for what you have done. The only thing I can give you is my embrace, dear Hanuman. Please accept my embrace. I am just offering myself unto you as a reward for that service.'

This is the highest gift we can give to God. Let us take inspiration from Hanuman and lead a life of selfless service.

Valuable Gifts

Human Quality: Satisfaction

In the holy town of Bhadrachalam in Telangana lived Raghuveer, a primary-school boy raised in a poor family. His father worked in the same school as a peon and his mother had become physically challenged after a road accident. His paternal grandmother stayed with them and helped with the domestic chores. He was consumed with distressing thoughts about his mother's physical condition and his family's financial state. His father's earnings were just about enough for two square meals a day and sometimes they even took loans. Raghu was always worried that he had nothing to give others, that made him feel isolated from his peers at school and instilled an inferiority complex in him. Over time, Raghu became disturbed.

As he was on his way home from school one evening, he saw a sage seated under a banyan tree. A Ram *bhakt*, he was always engaged in chanting of the names of Lord Ram. One look at the sage and one could experience serenity and peace within one's heart. His face was effulgent, and his words were replete with deep philosophical knowledge. Raghu felt drawn to the sage; he felt deeply inspired by his demeanour and wanted to seek advice from him. With his mind crowded by a barrage of depressing thoughts, he saw in the sage an able counsellor and someone he could trust.

'Namaste, Swamiji,' Raghu addressed the sage.

'Jai Shi Ram,' the sage responded with a chant of Lord Ram.

'Jai Shri Ram,' Raghu reciprocated.

'What's your name, young boy and what do you do?'

'I am Raghuveer, and I study in the fifth standard.'

'Jai Shri Ram,' the sage chanted again, recognizing that the boy was named after Lord Ram. 'How are you feeling today? How can I help you?'

'Swamiji, I am feeling very low'

'Hey Ram!' the sage exclaimed. 'Why so? What makes you, such a young boy, feel troubled?'

'I have problems in my family,' he began explaining the state of affairs in his family. As they conversed, the sage helped Raghu gain a different perspective.

As the conversation progressed, Raghu said, 'I have a desire to give to others, but unfortunately, I am so poor. I do not know whether I can actually contribute anything to others.'

The sage took pity on the young boy.

'I feel morose,' Raghu continued, 'because of my poverty and my inability to give anything to others.'

With compassion flooding his eyes, the sage tapped the young boy and said, 'My dear Raghu, you cannot imagine what gifts you already have. With this, you can give so much and delight others.'

'Really?' Raghu exclaimed with happiness. 'But I have no wealth or possessions.'

'Wealth is just one of things you can give,' the sage comforted Raghu. 'Just count the many other gifts that you can give others.'

'What are they, Swamiji?'

'The first gift you can give others is the gift of acceptance. Accept others the way they are.'

These words opened Raghu's mind to a new thought process.

'The second gift,' the sage continued, 'that you can give people is the gift of a great example: you can set a great example so that others can follow you. You can give others the gift of gratitude. You can give others the gift of transformative habits. For example, give up a bad habit which annoys others and when people see that, they will really be transformed.'

Raghu listened with rapt attention to the wisdom overflowing from the sage's lotus mouth.

'You want to give others one more gift? Please give them the gift of listening. Listen to them actively, invest in relationships by giving them your time, express your love for them. The gift of love is something which will touch their hearts. Give them the gift of teaching them some of your most valuable cherished realizations. Teach them what you know and what you want them to know. Most importantly, please know that the greatest gift you can give to anyone is accepting what they have to give you and share with you. Accept with a grateful heart.'

This gave Raghu a lot of clarity and he bowed down to the sage.

'You have so many gifts already,' the sage concluded. 'Please give these to people without any discrimination.'

'Thank you very much, Swamiji,' Raghu said with folded hands.

'*Ayushman Bhava*, may Ram bless you well.'

In the *Chaitanya Charitamrita* (Madhya 8.73), it is said:

> *mora karma, mora hāte-galāya bāndhiyā*
> *ku-viṣaya-viṣṭhā-garte diyāche phelāiyā*
> *vāmana yaiche cāṅda dharite cāhe kare*
> *taiche ei vāṣchā mora uṭhaye antare*

Many times, we indulge in activities which are self-destructive and therefore we should know that human life is rare and the choices we make today define our future. Let us not be under the illusion that we own nothing. Between the choices we make and our ability to desire, think, feel and will, we can transform the entire planet simply through our willpower and the desire to transform ourselves and others.

Let us do a cause-and-effect analysis along with discussing a solution to a fundamental problem we encounter in life, our ever-increasing desires.

THE PROBLEM: EVER-INCREASING DESIRES

There is a phenomenon in today's world of 'ever-increasing desires'. Our desires are unlimited but the supply of assets is limited. For this circumstance to work, we make rules, regulations, policies, state laws, etc. Perhaps you are reading this book with a hope to achieve inner peace and satisfaction.

You are not alone in this endeavour. In fact, all of us have been searching for it since time immemorial, but only a few fortunate ones crack the code on how to obtain that ultimate state of deep, undisturbed peace. Nothing in this world comes for free, and there is always a price to pay.

CAUSE OF DISSATISFACTION: GREED

As souls, we are *sat-cit-ananda*, eternal, full of knowledge and ever-blissful. But once we are conditioned by our material surroundings, there is a particular aspect of our contaminated consciousness that gives us dissatisfaction and also acts as hurdle to completely experiencing God's grace. This dissatisfaction and hindrance of bliss are due to the fuming greed in our hearts to own and rule both, people and life situations.

The cause of greed is simple. According to the Bhagavad Gita and the *Srimad Bhagavatam*, the origin of greed (*lobha*) is the mode of passion. As per lassical Vedic theology, greed originated from the lips of Brahma at the beginning of creation.

The first cause of greed is our propensity to enjoy. This enjoyment attitude dictates to mind, 'I want to enjoy and satisfy myself.'

Secondly, the desire to enjoy is supplemented by the egocentric attitude, 'I can and I have the power to fulfil my desire.'

When this desire is not fulfilled, it results in anger. But your calculation would be wrong if you think that desire, when fulfilled, results in satisfaction. No, it doesn't. It merely fuels the desire further. And finally, this hankering attitude manifests in greed as we keep desiring more and more.

SOLUTION: CONTROL AND CONQUER THE GREED

The *Srimad Bhagavatam* (7.15.22) says:

> *asankalpāj jayet kāmam,*
> *krodham kāma-vivarjanāt*
> *arthānartheksayā lobham*
> *bhayam tattvāvamarśanāt*

Through determination one shall conquer lust, and by giving up sense objects one shall conquer anger. By discussing the disadvantages of accumulating wealth one shall give up greed, and by discussing the truth one gives up fear.

Illusion is to think that money or sense gratification can bring us satisfaction. There is more to life than the tendency to possess external objects.

There was an old couple betting on horses in a race. Luckily, they won the lottery and received a cheque. The husband saw the number of zeroes in the cheque and he couldn't believe he was going to become super-rich. In that shock, he had a heart attack. The cheque was flying away from his hand. The wife had the worst dilemma: whether to catch her husband or the cheque. Such is the nature of money. It causes anxiety when it comes and distress when it goes away. This creates a hankering; we think we need money to finally be at peace but that's a fallacy. Scratching an itch can feel nice for some time, but the itch simply grows stronger. Unless we resist it, we can't overcome the problem. We should rather resist than persist.

All we need has already been provided by God in the form of the necessities of life. There is no point in acquiring more than we already have. This urge to be supported by external security measures represents the innate longing of the heart to truly feel fulfilled. This longing can only be satisfied through acts of selfless love for the Supreme Lord and his subjects. That alone can shower rain over the forest fire of burning material desires. Satisfaction of the heart is achieved by one who seeks refuge in God, as experiencing the love of God is the only true need of the soul.

TWENTY

Intelligence Is Power

Human Quality: Wisdom

In the Mewar kingdom, there was a minister who was very dear to the king. The king had a lot of confidence and faith in the minister's ability to analyse complex situations and advise him. As a result of their closeness, there were a bunch of other ministers who were envious. The king, on the other hand, was very kind and understanding of people's issues and was also approachable.

One day, when his intelligent minister reported sick, the envious ministers approached the king and put forward their concern, 'Your Highness, we feel discriminated against.'

'Why so, ministers?' the king probed.

'We see that you give importance to one minister over all of us.'

'I see,' the king nodded.

Another minister added, 'We work hard too, we have certain powers but it looks like you are much too inclined to this one minister.'

'I understand your concern,' the king affirmed. 'Well, it requires a certain degree of intelligence, the power to reason and deep analysis on certain tricky issues to be a good minister. Although I would like to have more such ministers, unfortunately, he is the only one who meets these criteria.'

'Sorry, Your Highness!' one minister politely disagreed, 'we don't think so. We can handle tough and tricky situations too.'

'All right,' the king said. 'Let me put you through one such situation.'

The ministers looked at each other and hesitantly agreed to the test.

'Please meet me at the lawn in an hour,' the king announced and left.

As the ministers gathered at the lawn, they saw the king standing next to an elephant from the royal entourage.

'Welcome, ministers,' the king gestured. 'Are you ready for the test?'

'Yes, Your Highness,' they responded in unison.

Pointing to the elephant, the king asked, 'What is the weight of this elephant?'

Before the ministers could ask a question, the king clarified, 'Tell me without using a weighing machine, of course.'

For a moment, the ministers were stumped. They remained speechless.

Sensing the confusion in the minds of the ministers, the king informed them that he would give them a day's time to think about it and solve the puzzle.

The ministers got together and all through the afternoon, evening and night thought of different ways in which they could approach the problem and solve it. They even contacted a few astrologers and veterinary doctors for advice. However, they were not able to solve the problem.

The next morning, the king arrived at the lawn along with his intelligent minister. The latter didn't have any context of what had happened the previous day and just followed the king.

The ministers honestly admitted to the king that they were unable to solve it.

The king smiled and looked at the intelligent minister right away, 'My dear minister, can you tell me what the weight of this elephant is without using a weighing machine?'

'Give me a few moments,' the minister said, after thinking it through for a moment.

'May I take the elephant with me for a while?' the minister asked the king.

'Yes, certainly.'

The minister left the scene with the elephant. However, within fifteen minutes, he returned with a wide smile on his face. That left the other ministers more anxious.

'My dear king,' the minister announced, much to the excitement of the other ministers. 'This elephant weighs 1920 kg.'

This truly bewildered everybody there.

'Did you use a weighing machine?' asked one of the envious ministers.

'Certainly not,' the minister assured, 'I measured with a boat.'

This confused all the ministers.

'Let me explain. I placed this elephant on a boat floating in water. I noticed the extent to which the boat dipped underwater. I marked that point on the sides of the boat.

Then, I made the elephant deboard. I started putting weights in the same boat and the moment the boat reached the same level, I stopped adding further weights.'

The envious ministers were simply amazed by the intelligence of this minister, and most importantly, his ability to think on his feet.

'This was 1920 kg,' the minister confirmed.

It is described in the *Srimad Bhagavatam* (4.20.3):

> sudhiyaḥ sādhavo loke
> naradeva narottamāḥ
> nābhidruhyanti bhūtebhyo
> yarhi nātmā kalevaram

Intelligent people utilize their brilliance for the purpose of gaining right character and protecting themselves from the miseries of this world, and ultimately reach that state which is beyond birth and death. Yes, all of us are under the influence of maya, the material energy, but we can prevent this by use of our intelligence. Let us ignite the power of intelligence to understand the discrimination between right and wrong, good and bad, beneficial and harmful and let us lead a life which will take us beyond dualities into the realm of eternal life.

In the *Chanakya Niti*, three signs of intelligent dealings are mentioned:

1. To speak according to the occasion

We should be very sensitive to the surroundings whenever we speak or express ourselves. This includes the circumstance, the audience and our state of mind too. To speak well is also to know when not to speak. For example, it's not advised to joke or laugh at a funeral. Similarly, it's not advised to cry at an auspicious occasion like a wedding. The reason such guidelines are given is because with our behaviour we emit energy, and it should not upset the ambience we are present in.

In the Bhagavad Gita (17.15), Krishna says,

anudvega-karaṁ vākyaṁ
satyaṁ priya-hitaṁ ca yat
svādhyāyābhyasanaṁ caiva
vāṅ-mayaṁ tapa ucyate

Austerity of speech consists of speaking words that are truthful, pleasing, beneficial and not agitating to others. It also involves regularly reciting Vedic literature. One should not speak in such a way so as to agitate the minds of others. Of course, when a teacher speaks, he/she can chide the students for their benefit, but such a teacher should not speak in the same way to those who are not their students if that will agitate their minds. This is penance as far as talking is concerned. Besides that, one should not talk nonsense. Talk should be pleasurable to the ear. Through such discussions, one may derive the highest benefit and elevate human society.

2. To render service as per ability

Having a service attitude is essential, but at the same time, we should take up responsibilities that match our capacity and capability. As far as capacity is concerned, it's a function of available bandwidth, as in, our ability to multitask and do justice to each task at the same time. As far as capability is concerned, it's a function of the degree of expertise required and whether we have the wherewithal (including all types of resources, monetary or otherwise) to do justice to the service or the responsibility picked up.

The core of the service attitude is sincerity and integrity. We should be fully committed to what we take up and strive for a 100 per cent say-to-do ratio in terms of timelines, quality of work and aligning with expected outcomes to be delivered.

3. **To exhibit anger no more than ability to influence**

We have seen that anger generally arises from contact with the three modes of material nature—goodness, ignorance and especially the mode of passion. When we act out of anger, *krodha vegam*, we are bound to do something we will regret later. We will say or do something that will cause us to be sorry, or experience sadness and grief in the long run. So, it is always best to avoid acting or speaking out of anger. Anger is effective when we exercise it in the right proportions, when we express it not in the first instance of an unfavourable outcome but only after a mistake is repeated. We should express anger only on issues within our circle of influence and only when such an expression can possibly better future outcomes.

TWENTY-ONE

What Is in a Donation?

Human Quality: Charity

Once, during His earthly pastimes, Lord Buddha was seated under a tree in Gaya and people in the locality began to offer charity for the saint. King Bimbisara led the gathering and came forward to offer grants of land, several gold coins and valuable jewels from his treasury. Lord Buddha extended his right hand and accepted it.

Prince Ajatshatru followed suit. He also offered several acres of land and other valuable gifts which Buddha accepted with his right hand again. Several prominent, wealthy merchants from the kingdom came forward and offered a lot of precious items in charity. Buddha accepted all that by extending his right arm.

Then an old lady came by. She looked completely dishevelled and poverty-stricken, and when she came for a darshan of Lord Buddha, she bowed down to him and Buddha reciprocated with respect.

'My dear lord,' she said, 'I am a poor lady, I have nothing much to offer.'

'Thank you for meeting me,' the Buddha said kindly.

'I was eating this pomegranate,' she said, pointing to it, 'and I had eaten half of it when I heard the news that you were accepting gifts of charity from citizens.'

Buddha smiled back.

'The remaining half is the only possession I have; I must give it to you. And therefore, please accept this offering of love which I have for you.'

Saying this she brought the half-eaten pomegranate in front of the Buddha. The Buddha came down from his seat to face her, and accepted it with both hands.

King Bimbisara was very surprised and so was Ajatshatru and the merchants assembled there.

'Lord Buddha,' King Bimbisara politely referred to the saint, 'when we offered various things, you just extended one hand but for this lady, you came down from your throne and accepted the half-eaten fruit with both hands.'

Lord Buddha nodded.

'But why?'

'Well . . .' Lord Buddha said, 'all of you gave whatever was as per your capacity in charity but as far as this lady is concerned, she gave everything that she had.'

The royal society looked at each other in wonder.

'She has given all of her possessions,' the saint continued, 'and has not held back anything for herself.'

Such a thought had never struck any of the citizens gathered there. The old woman had given all she had.

'Because she is giving her everything to me,' Buddha announced, 'I am also giving myself to her completely.'

To be in the mood of giving is a great thing and it is not always easy to cultivate.

In the *Srimad Bhagavatam* (10.22.35), Krishna talks to his cowherd friends, showing them the trees; Krishna glorifies the trees as follows:

etāvaj janma-sāphalyaṁ
dehinām iha dehiṣu
prāṇair arthair dhiyā vācā
śreya-ācaraṇaṁ sadā

The success of one's life is that one is able to offer one's body, mind, words, wealth, one's very life in the service of the Supreme Lord. Let us not be in anxiety while giving and know that the person who will benefit the most through giving is us. Let us get into the mood of selfless service and transform our life and the lives of others through these acts of charity.

Giving in charity purifies the heart because it helps us become detached from material things and cleanses the desire for favourable results. Giving in charity purifies our finances and accumulated wealth. If we envision the vast universe as a bank, the charity we give is like a deposit in that bank, the dividends being the purification of our hearts or the unexpected provision of our needs. Giving in charity allows us to put our money where our heart is. If our heart is in becoming God-conscious, in supporting activities centred around God, in knowing that the sincere practice of Krishna consciousness is good for the whole world, then we can show it by how we faithfully and regularly we give and do our part to ensure that such a mission spreads globally and is maintained well. That way, giving in charity pleases Krishna and increases our faith.

In the Bhagavad Gita (17.20–17.22), Krishna explains the various types of charity. Charity in the mode of goodness is given out of duty, at the proper time and place, to a worthy person and without expectation of return. Charity performed while expecting some return or in a grudging mood is said to be in the mode of passion. Charity performed at an improper place and time and given to unworthy persons, without respect and with contempt, is in the mode of ignorance and yields negative results or consequences.

The nectar of instruction discusses certain important principles we should keep in mind as we cultivate a charitable mind:

- Everything belongs to Krishna therefore, when we offer something in the service of the Lord, we're just returning the property to its rightful owner.
- Giving gifts, *prasadam*, money, time, and talent is a way to show love. It is one of the six loving exchanges between devotees. Spiritual life is a culture of giving.
- Giving charity is a sacrifice that purifies one's wealth. If wealth is not purified, it will be depleted through legal fees, medical bills, taxes, theft and so on.
- Even a little amount given in the service of God rewards the giver hundreds and thousands of times.

Ultimately, giving in charity is good for the soul and gives much benefit to the giver. Srila Prabhupada, the founder of the ISKCON Society, writes: 'What the devotee actually offers to the Lord is not needed by the Lord. He is self-sufficient. If the devotee offers something to the Lord, it acts in his own interest because whatever is offered comes back a million times greater. One does not become a loser by giving to the Lord, but he becomes a gainer a million times over.'

TWENTY-TWO

Transformation through Association

Human Quality: Association

Nestled between the Kaveri River on one side and its distributary Kollidam on the other, in the Trichy district of south India, is the river island Srirangam. Srirangam is home to the famous Shri Ranganatha Swamy temple, considered first among the 108 *divya desam* temples of Lord Vishnu. These divya desam temples have been visited and praised by the twelve Alvar saints of Tamil Nadu. This temple town bustles with activity through the year, with multitudes of devotees flocking for the Lord's magnificent darshan. Besides the presence of Shri Ranganatha Swamy, the divinity in the ambience is further bolstered with the constant chanting of the Lord's names by the devotees in *satsang* groups along with the frequent conduct of harikatha, a form of traditional discourse in which the storyteller explores a story from an Indian epic like the Ramayana and the Mahabharatha.

Once upon a time in the early 1970s in Srirangam, a *Bhagavata Saptaha* was organized as part of Krishna Janmashtami celebrations. As the name suggests, it is a seven-day discourse on the *Srimad Bhagavatam*. A famous

Vaishnava sage known to be an intellectual and a powerful speaker was invited to speak at the event for three hours daily. The news of this event spread fast to the nearby localities. One such locality is Lalgudi, which lay north-east of Srirangam across the Kollidam River, and there lived Muthu along with his wife on his ancestral property which was over a hundred years old. A tailor by profession, he was a workaholic and never pursued anything beyond his occupation, so much so that he failed to even care for the parrot that they kept at home. More often than not, his wife or mother had to remind him to feed the parrot throughout the day. His mother was a pious lady and ever since her husband passed away, she became fully engaged in chanting the holy names of Shri Hari.

As soon as the news of the harikatha event reached her, she felt happy and became keen to attend the sessions daily. The sessions were held in the evening, so she needed someone to accompany her as it would get late in the night by the time she returned. She had no one but her son, Muthu, to depend on. Although Muthu restricted himself to work-related engagements and was totally uninterested in spiritual topics, he had to oblige her request considering her safety. India in the 1970s, especially in small towns, was not home to as many cars as we see on the roads today. People had to travel on the state transport buses that plied at limited frequency. His mother thought she would use this opportunity to advise Muthu to look beyond work, gain knowledge in spiritual topics and evolve as a person. He reluctantly agreed to sit through the sessions at the saptaha.

They attended the sessions together. While Muthu's mother was contemplative, Muthu remained least interested. He would sometimes doze off during the sessions. On the contrary, his mother would reflect on some of the topics at the dinner table daily and share her perspectives on how one could apply them in life. This fell on Muthu's deaf ears, while the caged parrot keenly heard the words of the old lady. As it kept hearing her patiently, it began to bob its head repeatedly and squawk continuously.

'Did you feed the parrot after we returned?' Muthu's mother asked him as he was stitching a pair of trousers.

'No,' he replied nonchalantly.

'I can see from its behaviour,' she replied unhappy.

Sensing her tone, Muthu reluctantly fetched a bowl of water for the parrot.

'Parrots are sensitive,' she warned, 'and don't like being repeatedly mistreated.'

Indifferent about the warning but more concerned about the three hours of work missed in the evening, Muthu returned to his tailoring machine in a jiffy.

Four days passed and over time, Muthu's mother realized that the parrot was more attentive to her reflections on the katha. The fifth evening arrived and after her daily chanting of Vishnu *Sahasranama*, she began recalling the previous day's discussion on the glories of Prahlada Maharaja. She was specifically intrigued by Prahalad's instructions to his demonic schoolmates. It was philosophically rich and guided one on putting the human form of life to best use to be liberated from this material world. As the parrot listened to her intently, it became curious. Just then, Muthu's mother instructed him to serve water to the parrot.

'Muthu,' the parrot called him, 'please ask the sage today how I can get liberated.'

'What?!' Muthu laughed at this question and moved on to sharing it as a joke with his mother.

As the mother–son duo returned home that evening, the parrot eagerly awaited the answer. As it put forth the question, Muthu laughed at it. This time, even louder. Sensing the seriousness in the parrot's question, Muthu's mother assured him of an answer the following day.

On the sixth evening, as soon as the discourse ended, on the insistence of his mother, Muthu went and personally met the sage.

The sage asked, 'Yes, young man, do you have any question?'

'Well,' Muthu responded, 'my parrot had a query for you'

'Parrot?' the sage quizzed. 'What is it?'

'How can he be liberated from the cage?'

After hearing the question, the sage fell down unconscious. Muthu and fellow attendees were shocked as they wondered what had just happened. Muthu's mother was deeply concerned about what had just happened to the sage while Muthu had begun to palpitate, already fearing what his question had caused. The organizers gathered around and requested people to clear the area.

When he returned home, the parrot was waiting in the cage. He went to that parrot and the parrot said, 'Did you ask the question?

Muthu said, 'Yes, I asked the question. But unfortunately, something ghastly happened.'

The parrot asked, 'What happened?'

Muthu said, 'As soon as I asked the sage the question, "How can my parrot be liberated?" he fell down unconscious and he could not even answer the question.'

The parrot said, 'No problem, I got the answer.'

The next day, when Muthu woke up and came to feed the parrot, to his surprise he found that the parrot was dead and thought, 'Oh! My god, what has happened? Why has the parrot now lost symptoms of life.'

Out of great concern, he opened the cage. As soon as he opened the cage, the parrot suddenly got up and flew to freedom. The man was totally aghast.

Muthu went running to the sage's ashram and he told the sage, with bated breath, 'Swamiji, I don't know what happened but yesterday when I asked you how the parrot could be liberated, you fell unconscious. I don't know what happened.'

The sage said, 'Well, you asked me a question. I gave you the answer. You did not understand the answer, but the parrot did because he managed to fake his death and ultimately flew to liberation.'

That got Muthu thinking.

'I just gave one small hint,' the sage continued, 'and the parrot understood the method for liberation. You are attending my discourses every day, yet you didn't get what I meant.'

Therefore, the purpose of spiritual events is not entertainment. The purpose is to hear the discouse attentively, apply it and be transformed. When it comes to spiritual knowledge, such an association ultimately helps us achieve liberation from the cycle of birth and death.

In the *Srimad Bhagavatam* (1.10.11), it is described:

> sat-saṅgān mukta-duḥsaṅgo
> hātuṁ notsahate budhaḥ
> kīrtyamānaṁ yaśo yasya
> sakṛd ākarṇya rocanam

In the association with pure devotees, when we hear the transcendental messages, that creates impact, and that impact purifies and transforms us.

1. Association offers a platform for redirecting our love towards Krishna by engaging in spiritual practices.
2. Spiritual culture focuses on absorption and minimizes all distractions.
3. In such a culture, both men and women focus on developing their latent spirituality.
4. We see each other as potential spiritual beings, not as potential sex objects.
5. Such a vision helps us to strive undistractedly for inner fulfilment.
6. The more we become spiritually fulfilled, the more liberated we are from the constant craving for sex.
7. When sexual fantasies no longer dissipate our mental energy, we become free to fully use our abilities and resources for our and other's holistic well-being.
8. Real liberalization is therefore decreasing the sexualization of our culture and participating in its re-spiritualization.

TWENTY-THREE

Sugary Desires

Human Quality: Greed

In the serene town of Rishikesh was a gurukula which offered primary education. The uniqueness of this gurukula was that it held a Q&A session daily. Here, the students were encouraged to ask questions that intrigued them, and the onus was on the teacher to clarify them, preferably with anecdotes or experiments. The curriculum was designed in such a way that students were also graded on both the quantity and the quality of questions they asked. The founding fathers of the gurukula also believed that such a practice of question hour together with regular field trips engage the millennial generation and approach using anecdotes or experiments makes learning scientific.

During one question hour, Vidya, a student in fourth grade asked the teacher, 'Madam, please tell me, what is the meaning of greed?'

The teacher thought for a moment and then said, 'On Friday, I will take you to a tour of a candy factory nearby.'

Vidya and the other students felt excited after this announcement.

'There,' the teacher continued, 'we will learn what greed is and much more. That will be your field trip this month.'

The students were thrilled and eagerly looked forward to the visit to the candy factory.

Friday arrived and the students reached the candy factory along with the teacher in the school van.

As they were about to begin the tour, Vidya gently reminded the teacher about her question about greed. The teacher tapped her shoulder and nodded in affirmation.

'Now,' she announced, 'as we enter the candy factory, you will see the assembly line of different varieties of candies.'

'Wow, this is so wonderful,' cheered bespectacled, curly-haired Anmol.

'I am so excited,' Vidya seconded. The reaction of the rest of the students was equally happy.

'But there is a rule,' the teacher said, 'as we walk through the candy factory, you are allowed to pick up only one candy.'

This dampened the students' spirit as they had other ideas in mind.

'Secondly,' she added, 'you cannot turn back. You can only go forward as we walk. Pick the sweet you like best.'

Then the teacher led the students into the factory. As they started walking through the assembly line, the students' mouth began to water looking at the rich variety of candy in varying sizes. Chocolate-covered strawberries, caramel popcorn, jellybeans, gummies, hard candies, lollipops, caramels and bonbons were the most delectable of options there.

With the condition in place, the students walked forward slowly and steadily, with an eye on what was coming up next, so as to pick the best candy available. Many a time they felt like picking up a candy but the fear of missing out of an even better one made them hesitate. They longed for the tastiest and largest candy available there.

'Hey, the next one looks bigger,' murmured one.

'I just missed the last one, I should have picked that up,' said an upset student.

'This one looks so tasty, maybe I should grab it,' wondered one.

Right through the walk along the assembly line, the students had various thoughts and experienced many conflicting emotions as they had to pick one sweet among many.

'We have come to the end of the assembly line now,' announced the teacher, leaving the students confused, 'there are no more candies.'

While some students had grabbed one, many left the assembly line empty-handed. Among the ones who had picked one, very few were happy with their choice; they wished they had waited for the ones to follow or had picked a preceding one.

'So,' the teacher asked another question, 'which candy did you choose?'

The students who had picked up a piece of candy raised their hands and showed the others what they had, while other students responded with the names.

'I kept waiting for the best one,' began one student, 'but never got one.'

'I should have picked the earlier one,' regretted another, 'but I missed it.'

The teacher smiled at all the students and said, 'Do you now understand what greed is?'

'Yes, ma'am,' was the thumping response from one and all.

She continued, 'That is the power of greed; it forces you to go beyond what is currently there and you begin looking for what you do not have.'

The students nodded.

'If you have learnt the lesson well,' the teacher added, 'I will surprise you now.'

'Yes, ma'am,' the students replied in unison.

'My rule was just for the lesson. Please go ahead and choose your favourite candies.'

'Thank you, ma'am,' the students screamed and rushed to the assembly line.

In the Bhagavad Gita (2.70), it is said:

> *āpūryamāṇam acala-pratiṣṭhaṁ*
> *samudram āpaḥ praviśanti yadvat*
> *tadvat kāmā yaṁ praviśanti sarve*
> *sa śāntim āpnoti na kāma-kāmī*

When a person is at peace within, when he is self-satisfied, such a state of self-satisfaction is like an ocean where the multiple rivers of desire cannot create any agitation and cannot shake the person. In this way, when we experience unlimited joy and satisfaction, that feeling of joy and satisfaction is the basis for realizing the real goal of our lives, which is not to indulge sense gratification but to engage in the service of the Supreme Lord and humanity. When we give up these tendencies towards greed, we understand that the real greed must be to obtain the ultimate spiritual realization. That greed is the currency through which the Supreme Lord becomes very easily attainable.

Let's discuss the seven ways to overcome greed. The acronym is SATISFY:

1. Serve others
2. Avoid meat-eating
3. Train your mind to focus on the principles of satisfaction
4. Insulate your intelligence with transcendental knowledge
5. Spiritualize your desires
6. Feast on Krishna Prasadam
7. Yield in front of God

SERVE OTHERS

The modern paradigm propels us to assume that if we don't acquire more, we're miserable and unworthy. This isn't true. Through giving, we receive more. Living a life of service to others fulfils our hearts and makes it purposeful, it drives us to share love with everyone without selfishness. Krishna was once telling his cowherd friends that trees are great personalities because the only purpose in their life is to serve others irrespective of the heat, cold, wind or any other eternal circumstances. With such tolerance, they still are willingly producing fruits and flowers for others and also provide refuge to birds, animals and humans at times.

The difference between animal and human bodies is that the animal body is useful even after death while humans are useful only until they're alive. Therefore, if you want to make your life useful and successful, four things are suggested by the scriptures: *pranayair arthair dhiya vaca*—pranayair, use your life; arthair, use your wealth; dhiya, use your intelligence; vaca use your words. For what? *Sreyan aca*—that is to do good for yourself and others by serving them.

AVOID MEAT-EATING

There are severe consequences of meat-eating. There are economic, health, environmental, moral and spiritual reasons that suggest that one must adapt to a diet filled with vitality. It is a widely known fact that all the cells in our body are completely replaced within a three-month period. Thus, whatever we eat becomes the building bricks of our system. The new cells get nutrition from what we eat. If we are trying to satisfy ourselves at the expense of someone else's life, how can there be any satisfaction within? We are trying to be peaceful by killing and slaughtering someone and it is quite foolish to think it is possible. Yes, the best way to become satisfied is to love and be loved. To develop compassion for other animals is one of the ways to share our love. But if insensitivity and indifference towards killing animals persist and blind our eyes from seeing dead corpses being served on our plates, such compassion cannot develop.

TRAIN YOUR MIND TO FOCUS ON THE PRINCIPLES OF SATISFACTION

> *sada santusta manasah*
> *sarvah sivamaya disah*
> *sarkara kantakhadibhyo*
> *yathopanat padah sivam*

'For a person who has suitable shoes on his feet, there is no danger even when he walks on pebbles and thorns. For him, everything is auspicious. Similarly, for one who is always self-satisfied, there is no distress; indeed, he feels happiness everywhere' (*Srimad Bhagavatam*, 7.15.17).

The feeling of satisfaction is like a cover protecting the mind just as a pair of shoes protect our feet. And our mind is protected when it is covered with contentment and happiness derived from such satisfaction. Success is getting what you like but satisfaction and happiness are liking what you get.

INSULATE YOUR INTELLIGENCE WITH TRANSCENDENTAL KNOWLEDGE

Intelligence misused is highly destructive. After protecting the mind with satisfaction, intelligence needs to be insulated with the transcendental knowledge of the Bhagavad Gita and *Srimad Bhagavatam*. Such scriptures bestow the feeling of gratitude towards the Supreme Lord and take us down the path of living a life of satisfaction.

SPIRITUALIZE YOUR DESIRES

Ice and water are made of the same components. Ice is the solid form and water, the liquid. However, they possess opposing qualities. Water has the power to make a heavy ship float while an iceberg possesses the power to drown the same ship. Likewise, our desires can be beneficial or irrevocably damaging to our consciousness. Thus, spiritualizing our desires is extremely important. Spiritualizing desires means changing the nature of our desire to enjoy to the desire to see others in joy. Acting from a place of selflessness and utilizing our desire in the service of the Lord, for His satisfaction, can bring us an immense feeling of contentment.

FEAST ON KRISHNA PRASADAM

How is it possible to feel satisfied when we are feasting like beasts? It is possible. In Krishna Consciousness, the way to attain satisfaction is by satisfying the Supreme Lord. One of the easiest ways to do that is by lovingly cooking delicacies from the fruits, vegetables and other raw ingredients provided by the Lord and offering it to him with devotion. When he tastes the food made with devotion and gratitude, he is completely satisfied. Since he resides within all of our hearts as *paramatma* or super soul, we too feel that satisfaction in return. After tirelessly cooking for the Lord, we can even experience almost no appetite because we worked simply for His pleasure and not for ours. By honouring the remnants of the Lord as prasadam, we lose interest in seeking material pleasures through our senses.

YIELD IN FRONT OF GOD

The final step is to yield in front of the Supreme Lord and surrender ourselves at his lotus feet. Submission to God is the safest pillow to rest on. Because when we submit our false ego and independence to the Lord, we are also accepting His desires as ours and agreeing to work under His will. By becoming the instrument of His sweet will, we please Him greatly. The concluding message of the Bhagavad Gita is '*Mam ekam saranam vraja*'. Krishna says to Arjuna to ultimately surrender unto him. In the age of Kali, Krishna in the form of Lord Chaitanya preached the chanting of the holy names of the Lord as the easiest way to surrender ourselves to God. Thus, the simple method of surrender is to chant the *Hare Krishna Mahamantra*—Hare Krishna, Hare Krishna, Krishna Krishna, Hare Hare, Hare Ram, Hare Ram, Ram Ram, Hare Hare!

TWENTY-FOUR

The Greatest Protection

Human Quality: Faith

Back in the thirteenth century CE, at the peak of a long-lasting war between the Chola and the Pandya kingdoms in South India, the Chola soldiers were heavily injured and seemed to be on the verge of defeat.

After one such battle, a young soldier was injured badly and started running away to save his life. The Pandya troops went chasing after him. With most of the Chola soldiers scattered and defeated, he hardly had support. Heavily bruised, with arrows piercing his knees, he managed to run up towards a mountain. As the Pandyas came chasing, he became desperate and found a cave. It seemed to be a safe hiding spot. He entered the cave and took refuge there. Yet, there he was anxious. He began to pray to the Lord who happened to be just a few miles away from where he was hiding: Lord Ranganath of Srirangam.

As fear of impending death engulfed him, he prayed more faithfully, 'Om Namo Narayana, my dear Lord, if somehow or the other You save me today, I assure you that

I will dedicate my life to Your service. And I shall serve at Your lotus feet in Srirangam.'

He went into a meditative state for a few minutes and prayed sincerely from the bottom of his heart. Wary of the surroundings, he opened his eyes to watch out for the movement of the enemy camp. Just then, all of a sudden, the enemy troops came near that cave and one of them started walking up to the cave. As the Chola soldier listened to the their movements, he saw a spider appear right in front of him. It went to the entrance of the cave and started making a web there.

When the young soldier saw this happen, he became anxious and also unhappy. He called out to the Lord, 'My dear Ranganath, I prayed to you for protection. Instead of sending me a huge army, you have sent an insignificant spider my way instead! How am I going to protect myself, Narayana? Are you not listening to my prayer?'

As he was exchanging his thoughts with the Lord, to make matters worse, the Pandya soldiers came closer. As he peeped out, he saw four of them, well-armed and charged up to take possession of him. As they looked around where to continue the search, one of them approached the entrance to the cave, and as he unveiled his sword, his eyes fell on the web created by the spider.

One glance at the network of the spiderweb, this soldier turned to the rest of the troop and said, 'Well, looks like nobody is inside.'

The Chola soldier felt relieved as he experienced this magic unravel right in front of his eyes.

'How do you say so?' the other soldiers asked.

'If someone was inside,' he continued, 'there would not be a spiderweb here. Let's head back.'

They were convinced and turned back.

The Chola soldier had tears in his eyes. He sat in deep meditation for a few more minutes, meditating on the form of Lord Ranganath. Later, as promised, he headed to Srirangam and dedicated his life to service of the Lord. Over time, drawing inspiration from life, he became a powerful preacher and spread the message of the love of God. He was often quoted as saying, 'When the Lord's will is there, a spider's web can become as powerful as a stone wall. And if the Lord's will is not there, even a stone wall becomes as weak and fragile as a spiderweb.'

In the *Srimad Bhagavatam* (1.15.5), it is said:

> *vañcito 'ham mahā-rāja*
> *hariṇā bandhu-rūpiṇā*
> *yena me 'pahṛtam tejo*
> *deva-vismāpanam mahat*

Arjuna is a powerful example of someone who was given terrific powers by the Lord. But at one point of time, even Arjuna's powers were withdrawn and he expressed his realization, saying, 'I understand that whatever I have are the assets gifted to me by the Lord and the Lord can take away these assets at any time.'

Therefore, let us not forget that whatever power has been given to us is an endowment and a gift from the Supreme Lord. Let us always be dependent on His will and try to please Him.

This story is a great example of what a sincere prayer recited with deep faith can do. Let's start with understanding what is faith. The word 'faith' is used to define trust or belief in someone or something, but more commonly it is used in association with religion and God. The English word faith originates from the latin *fideis* which comes from the ancient Greek word *pistis*.

As people place their faith in scientific conclusions and evolutionary theories, they fail to take many things into account. If one observes the method in which scientific research is conducted, it generally begins with various theories and presuppositions—almost everything is changeable or disposable. Scientific theories have been revised, rethought and proven wrong throughout history. To place one's faith in this guessing game can be a disappointing venture.

We, as humans, are limited by the senses that our body is equipped with. People relate so much with their bodies and senses that it becomes almost impossible for them to think outside of the small realm of experience they have access to. The senses are only able to perceive things that are situated in the realm of physical matter.

According to the Vedic way of thinking there are four defects present in all people:

1. *Bhrama*: We are subject to illusion. This means that we may perceive one thing to be another. A classic example of this is someone who sees a rope lying on the ground and mistakes it for a snake. This kind of illusion also extends to one's own self. We experience illusion about our identity. We have forgotten our spiritual position

and have begun to identify ourselves with our temporary, mortal body.

2. *Pramada*: We have the tendency to make mistakes. Everyone makes mistakes arising from carelessness or inattention. When we are not focused on a particular task we end up making mistakes.

3. *Vipralipsa*: We have the desire to deceive. This desire arises when one finds it advantageous to exploit someone or withhold the truth from another.

4. *Karanapatva*: We have imperfect senses. Every single one of our senses is limited. Each sense organ is limited to one function (our eyes can only see, our ears can only hear, etc.). Even with the limited function they are meant to perform, they are defective. The capacity of our senses is greatly impaired by different circumstances (insufficient light or the distance of an object from the viewer). Even under ideal circumstances these senses can provide imperfect information.

In Sanskrit the word for faith is *sraddha*. Sraddha comes from two root words *srat* and *dadhati*, meaning that which leads to truth and reality. There are two types of faith to be obtained by the individual. One is transcendental faith (*paramarthika sraddha*) and the other is mundane faith (*laukika sraddha*). If one places one's faith in mundane knowledge, it will be tainted with the defects of human nature listed above.

The Vedic scriptures detail three ways in which a person attains knowledge. The first and most common is called *pratyaksa* or direct perception. Much of our basic learning comes from direct experience of the world around us. Pratyaksa is external (knowledge acquired through the senses) as well as internal (emotions perceived within ourselves such as pain, pleasure, love and hate). Everyone accepts pratyaksa as a valid medium with which to obtain knowledge but it is not always reliable for several reasons. It is limited to the present (you cannot have direct experience of the past or the future), it is limited to material things (spiritual elements cannot be perceived with material perception) and it is also limited by our imperfect senses.

The second is called *anumana* or inference. This means to reach a conclusion based on evidence, reasoning and prior experience. There is an example in the Vedas of a fire on the mountain. One sees smoke rising from the mountainside and concludes that there is a fire on the mountain.

There are five steps taken in order to reach this conclusion:

1. *Pratijna* (proposition): There is a fire on the mountain.
2. *Hetu* (reason): Because it is smoky.
3. *Udaharana* (general principle and example): Where there is smoke there is fire.
4. *Upanaya* (application): There is smoke over the mountain.
5. *Nigamana* (conclusion): Therefore, there is a fire on the mountain.

Through the evidence at hand, reasoning and prior experience, a person will reach the conclusion that there is a fire on the mountain despite not seeing the fire.

This process is also not free of faults because it still involves the imperfect senses. One could mistake a fog bank or cloud to be smoke. If the sense perception is wrong, then the conclusion will also be wrong.

Then the third is called *sabda*. Sabda means to hear from a person who is a trustworthy authority on a particular subject matter. Sabda can refer to any authority on any subject (i.e., a history teacher is an authority on the subject of history). However, a deeper meaning of sabda refers to knowledge of reality that is coming from a reliable source free from the four defects of human nature. This is known as *apauruseya sabda*, meaning it has no human origin and is untainted by material defects. Apauruseya also means that which is eternally existing without beginning. The Vedic literatures are apauruseya as they are handed down through an unbroken chain of disciples from their eternal and untainted source, Krishna. This is the strong link to pure knowledge.

TWENTY-FIVE

Pleasure Is an Exchange

Human Quality: Devotion

A sculptor was seen sculpting two beautiful *murtis* of Lord Krishna playing on his flute in His *tribhanga* form. As he meditated on the form of the Lord, trying to chip every little stone correctly, his friend walked in.

'Why are you making two deities?' he exclaimed.

The sculptor came out of a state of trance, and it took him a moment to gather what his friend had asked.

'What is it?' the sculptor asked.

'Why are you making two deities?' he repeated. 'Why can't you make just one deity?'

'Well, you see that place,' the sculptor pointed to a raised position on the wall, 'you see this pillar, we are going to place this deity right on top of that pillar.'

'Well, that's OK,' his friend nodded, 'but even in that case, why do you need two? One is sufficient.'

'Actually, we need only one,' he agreed, 'but as I was sculpting this first deity, I dragged the knife on the face accidentally, and there is a scratch under the nose.'

He went closer to the deity and showed it to his friend.

His friend took a closer look at what must have been about 2 cm long mark.

'I get it,' his friend continued, 'but this is such a tiny scratch.'

The sculptor smiled.

'And,' the friend continued, 'if it is such a tiny scratch and the murti is going to be placed right up there, who will be able to see it?'

'Yes, it's not visible to the naked eye,' the sculptor affirmed.

'If nobody can notice it there, why don't you just place this one there?'

'But . . .' the sculptor began.

'What's the need for a second one?'

'No ordinary human being will be able to detect this,' the sculptor asserted, 'but the Supreme Lord is all knowing, He sees everything. He sees everyone. I am sculpting this murti to please Him.'

'My God!' his friend exclaimed, understanding the gravity of thought and sincerity in intent.

'Krishna should be satisfied,' the sculptor concluded, 'and I will do whatever it takes to please Him.'

The friend saluted the sculptor's spirit of devotion.

In the *Srimad Bhagavatam* (1.19.15), Maharaj Parikshit prays to the Lord:

> *taṁ mopayātaṁ pratiyantu viprā*
> *gaṅgā ca devī dhṛta-cittam īśe*
> *dvijopasṛṣṭaḥ kuhakas takṣako vā*
> *daśatv alaṁ gāyata viṣṇu-gāthāḥ*

'My dear Lord, my dear sages, please go on chanting the wonderful glories of Krishna. And I am sitting here. Even if the snake-bird Takshak comes and bites me, I have nothing to fear because I am doing the right thing.'

Let us try to meditate on doing the right thing always. It's important that we live every moment of life in an absorbed state, after having understood that the Supreme Lord sees everything, hears everything, senses everything, including the deepest and minutest layers of our intentions. He knows it all, truly! As they say, the essence of integrity is what we do when no one watches us.

Living a God-centred life with this understanding is the foundation of spirituality.

Let's discuss the four principles of spirituality:

1. **Humility**

    a. **The first requirement to receive knowledge**

    Srila Prabhupada, the founder acharya of ISKCON, explained humility as freedom from the anxiety of having 'the satisfaction of being honoured by others'. Pride, the opposite of humility, makes us crave honour from others as our source of happiness.

    One should approach the spiritual master with humility and offer him all services so that he is pleased to bestow his blessings upon the disciple. As a bona fide spiritual master is a representative of Krishna, if he bestows any blessings upon his disciple, that will make the disciple spiritually advanced immediately. Humility keeps the heart fertile to receive spiritual knowledge.

b. **Without humility all spiritual efforts are wasted**

One may wonder, why bother to be humble when life goes on anyway, specifically when the world tends to exploit those who are meek and good-hearted? Why be the victim when we can win over others and live a great life?

The fact is that genuine humility is the secret key to all success in life. Remember: there is always at least one person in the world who is better than you. A humble blade of grass survives even the most powerful storm because it is willing to bend. Humility teaches us to respect time, the invincible. With humility comes tolerance which, along with determination, raises one to newer heights. Humility encourages honesty, gratitude and inner bliss. It delivers lasting happiness as one rises above mundane competition and hankering. Those who have successfully cultivated it can not only appreciate its full value but can also make others experience it. This is the beauty of true humility. It can have a ripple effect in generating other divine qualities and steers our efforts towards spiritual progress.

c. **You mean what you desire**

One can think of humility as weakness, such as, 'If I am humble, people will walk all over me'. Such an understanding arises from a misunderstanding of humility. Actual humility is not about looking down on us but about looking up at something bigger than ourselves. When we face challenges in life, especially challenges that are beyond what we can face on our own, we learn the power of humility. If we aren't humble, we are left with nothing except our own inadequate power. But if we are humble, we can seek help from some power bigger than ourselves. The biggest power is God, Krishna. And humility frees us from self-consciousness and empowers us to rise to God consciousness. Further, if we give shape to desires aligned with the above thought process, it takes us closer to God and helps us grow spiritually. Our desires should be shaped by our real intent and not fanned by the motives or influence of others. We should truly mean what we desire. When there is alignment in thoughts, words and actions, there is integrity, honesty and humility. This gives rise to other godly qualities in the individual.

2. **Simplicity**

a. **Reconnect to the natural course of life**

Modern civilization has advanced materially, medically and technologically. It has certainly increased lifespan, introduced more technologically advanced gadgets, faster modes of transportation and rapid methods of communication. However, life has also become more complicated and our attachment to gadgets like mobile phones and smart watches is evident. This affects our mental satisfaction and overall quality of life.

Simplicity means reconnecting with the natural course of life. This is to stay closer to nature and find happiness in the smallest of things creation has bestowed upon us.

b. **Decrease artificial necessities**

The necessities of life are food, water, air and shelter. With present-day modernization, we have increased our necessities manifold and instilled a sense of attachment to them. Here are a few statistics from a research conducted in 2023 that should help us get a sense of reality.[*]

♦ 47 per cent of parents surveyed believe their child has a smartphone addiction.

♦ Of the teachers surveyed, 67 per cent noticed their students being negatively distracted by mobile devices.

♦ In the eighteen- to twenty-nine-year-old category, 22 per cent of smartphone-using respondents admitted to checking their device every few minutes.

♦ Adults spend an average of forty-five minutes a day on social media alone.

♦ Rather than in-person interaction, 33 per cent of teens spend more time socializing with close friends online.

To foster simplicity, it's important that we reduce artificial necessities. This is not to say that we should stay away from mobile phones. Yes, times have changed and so have our ways of life.

c. **Increase austerity to improve health**

Modern civilization, on the pretext of making life easy, has made people less active. Walking has been

---

[*] '44 Smartphone Addiction Statistics for 2023', SlickText Blog, 23 January 2023, https://www.slicktext.com/blog/2019/10/smartphone-addiction-statistics/.

replaced by bicycles, bicycles by motorcycles, outdoor games by video games. Besides, the invention of electronic appliances like mixers and grinders, the fondness for mobiles and other electronic gadgets have added to the situation. It's important that we regulate some of these activities and not get addicted to gadgets. They have implications on our physical health. In the context of spirituality, austerity means voluntarily accepting difficult conditions for a higher purpose. We begin austerity by trying to stop exploiting material resources as if we own them. This means we must learn tolerance because the material energy rarely acts for our comfort in the long run. Numerous little things in life irritate us. The more attached we are to physical ease, the more troublesome these things become.

3. **Humanity**

   a. **Avoid the propensity to cheat**

   Many times, we come across promising relationships which go on peacefully for a while but suddenly suffer a major jolt and end, mostly due to problems related to money or infidelity. This stems from the propensity to cheat. We have a tendency to grab that which does not rightfully belong to us. And due to this, when we encroach upon another's property, there is unnecessary tussle and fight. When we try to grab another person's wealth, we are not just grabbing that person's property, we are trying to steal from the Supreme Lord Hari Himself. In the *Shri Isopanishad*, it is said:

īśāvāsyam idaṁ sarvaṁ yat kiñca jagatyāṁ jagat
tena tyaktena bhuñjīthā mā gṛdhaḥ kasya svid dhanam

Everything animate or inanimate that is in the universe is controlled and owned by the Lord. One should therefore accept only those things which are necessary and set aside as his quota, and one should not accept other things, knowing well to whom they belong.

Let us be satisfied with what we have and Krishna will provide us more than what we deserve.

b. **Embrace positive habits**

We become what we do repeatedly. Therefore habits can either make us or break us. Nearly 90 per cent of our daily activities are based on our habits. There can be two types of habits—physical (such as watching TV) or mental/attitudinal (such as worrying too much). We must consciously create the right kind of habits and nourish them. Simultaneously, we must avoid creating new bad habits and break our existing bad habits with determination. A strong person is someone who has successfully conquered bad habits.

Habits are formed by the repetition of particular acts. If an act is performed for approximately thirty-one days or so, it becomes a habit. From the Vedas, we find an excellent treatise on yoga contained in the yoga *sutras* of Patanjali. According to it, the mechanisms of habits can be understood based on the following concepts:

- *citta* (consciousness, heart or mind)
- *klesa* (hindrances/afflictions of the mind)
- *vritti* (thought, emotion, sensation or idea)
- *samskara* (sensory impressions or imprints made on citta)
- *karma* (our actions)

c. **Stick to ancient values**

Our ancient Vedic values are highly scientific, and their intent was to keep things natural and closer to God and *satvik* lifestyle. In recent years, we have observed how the world has begun to adopt and find value in the Vedic lifestyle with the adoption of yoga, ayurveda, *siddha*, etc. As we all know, India is home to ancient temples. There is a reason why such temples were built and why visiting temples continues to be a habit even today. Let's scientifically look at it.

Magnetic and electric waves are constantly moving inside the earth. When a temple is built, architects and engineers choose a piece of land where these waves are abundant. The main deity is placed in the centre of the temple; this place is also known as sanctum sanctorum. After the temple is built, the deity is erected, the worship of which is commonly known as *pranapratishta*. The deity is placed where the magnetic waves are highly active. During the installation of the deity, they bury some copper plates under the statue. These plates are engraved with the Vedic script, and they absorb magnetic waves from the earth and radiate them to the surrounding area. Therefore if a person regularly visits the temple and moves around the deity clockwise, his body absorbs these magnetic waves which increases the positive energy to live a healthy life.

This is just one instance of the scientific nature of the Vedic lifestyle. Should we continue to embrace ancient values, we will become more humane.

4. **Community**

a. **Share knowledge with next generation**

One of the reasons why ancient Vedic knowledge and traditional lifestyle is adopted less in modern times is because of the knowledge not being passed on as well. As parents and elders in the family, we have a responsibility to communicate the importance of why we do what we do to the next generation. That way, there will be continuity in practice, and we should do this for the welfare of our family and well-being of our lineage.

b. **Protect children from bad habits**

Modern civilization and the advent of the internet and technology has also facilitated rampant moral pollution. It's very important that parents strike a fine balance between being watchful and giving freedom to children. Regulating children's behaviour is very important.

c. **Inspire them through your example**

For us to succeed in driving the right behaviours in children we have to walk the talk. The best form of leadership is to lead by example. When we do what we expect of them, they find us credible. This includes practices like rising early in the morning, dedicated time for daily prayers, regulated use of mobile phones, showing kindness to elders in the family, focusing on maintain good physical health, staying away from junk food, etc.

TWENTY-SIX

Motherly Respect

Human Quality: Purposefulness

In the Nanda dynasty, there lived a king who went on a journey with his minister. As they went they travelled, they came across a tulsi plant. Over seven feet high, it had grown exceptionally. The devout minister bowed down and offered his obeisance.

'Why are you bowing down in front of a plant?' asked the sceptical king.

'My dear king, she is my mother.'

'How's that supposed to be?' asked the king with smirk.

He then plucked a leaf from the plant and asked the minister, 'How many mothers do you have?'

'She is tulsi, our mother,' the minister humbly replied, 'and therefore we worship her.'

Not convinced with his heart permeated with pride, the king moved ahead on the chariot with the minister following him. After a few metres' distance, the minister bowed down to another plant. This enraged the king.

'What's wrong with you?' he shouted at the minister. 'Who is this now?'

'This is my father,' the minister replied, pointing to an ivy plant which was poisonous and known to cause an itch.

The king became angry and pulled at the plant with his hands. However, as soon as he touched the plant, his hands started itching.

Enraged, the king said, 'Hey, my hands are itching, do something about it. Why did this happen?'

The minister smiled and replied, 'Because you were angry with the mother, the father got angry and hence he has given you this reaction.'

The king said, 'Not the time to debate right now, do something. This itching sensation is spreading all over my body.'

'Yes, there is a solution' the minister replied calmly.

'What is the solution?' the king asked.

'You have to take the blessing of another mother.'

'Which mother?' the king asked with bated breath.

Immediately, the minister pointed to the cow.

'Is the cow a mother too?' the king asked, half-disgusted.

'Yes,' the minister said. 'Mother Kamadhenu.'

'Anyway, no time for discussion,' the king ran to the cow, 'help me '

The minister applied cow dung on the body of the king. Although uncomfortable with what was happening, he immediately experienced relief from the itching.

'I'm feeling better now,' the king said, 'but . . .'

'But what, Your Highness?' the minister asked.

'How am I going to enter the palace like this?' the king asked, pointing to the dung all over the body.

'There is one more solution.'

'Phew! What's that?'

'You have to take the blessing of another mother.'

'One more mother? Which mother?'

The minister pointed to the flowing river nearby, Mother Ganga and said, 'Please jump into Mother Ganga.'

Therefore, as far as those who are practising *sanatana* dharma are concerned, tulsi, cow and Ganga are our venerable mothers.

And so, it is described:

> *āhāra-nidrā-bhaya-maithunaṁ ca*
> *sāmānyam etat paśubhir narāṇām*
> *dharmo hi teṣām adhiko viśeṣo*
> *dharmeṇa hīnāḥ paśubhiḥ samānāḥ*

The difference between animal and human consciousness is that humans have the capacity to understand the value and purpose of life. Humans have the capacity to understand that the goal of life is not simply eating, sleeping, mating and defending, but to realize the divinity within. By connecting with the Supreme Divine, we are able to see the divinity within all living beings.

The purpose of life can be accomplished balancing two qualities:

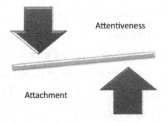

There are three parameters to consider while balancing attentiveness and attachment:

1. Vision: The attached are oblivious to the big picture and the attentive are aware of the background of spiritual reality.
2. Driver: The attached are driven by feelings, emotions and sentiments without discrimination. The attentive are driven by spiritual intelligence, clearly understanding the need and purpose behind any endeavour.
3. Success: The attached evaluate success based on outcomes and result. They become elated by the ups and depressed by the downs of life. The attentive focus on crafting a perfect endeavour, doing everything in their control to make the best attempt possible. They foster a growth mindset within.

TWENTY-SEVEN

The Bigger Hands

Human Quality: Faith

A father went to a sweet shop along with his son. The sweet-shop owner was very pleased to see the boy and he said kindly, 'Boy, I'm so glad to see you.'

'Thank you, uncle,' the boy smiled.

'I want to gift you something. Please bring your hands forward. I want to put some candy in your hands.'

The boy did not respond and kept looking at his dad.

The father interjected, 'My dear son, see, uncle is so merciful, so kind. He is asking you to place your hands in front of him.'

Yet the son didn't respond and kept looking at the father.

The father looked at the son and said, 'My dear son, please respond. See how this uncle is asking you to place your hands in front.'

The boy just smiled and hid himself behind the father and kept looking at him.

Finally, the father, of his own accord, placed his own hand forward and the sweet-shop owner picked up the candies and placed it in the father's hands.

As they headed out of the shop, the father asked the son, 'My dear son, the sweet-shop owner was asking you again and again to place your hands in front of you. Why didn't you do that?'

'For the simple reason, Dad,' he quickly responded, 'that your hands are bigger than mine. And so, your hands can accommodate a larger number of sweets than my hands.'

In the Bhagavad Gita (7.7), Krishna says:

> *mattaḥ parataraṁ nānyat*
> *kiñcid asti dhanañ-jaya*
> *mayi sarvam idaṁ protaṁ*
> *sūtre maṇi-gaṇā iva*

Everything in this creation comes from the Supreme Lord. He is the ultimate origin of all, therefore let us be dependent on Him because dependence on Him gives us greater benefits than trying to understand what we can do with our limited capacity and understanding independent of His supreme, divine will.

The story above is a lesson on how the boy established his relationship with his father and acknowledged that it is better to receive life's gifts from his hands. Similarly, if we, as children of God, acknowledge our direct relationship with the Supreme Lord and see every gift in life as given by His lotus hands, we stand to gain too.

For that to happen, we need to get over five types of disturbances or *klesas* that cause impediment in building the right identity as children of God.

AVIDYA—IGNORANCE

Ignorance is considering the soul to be the body. Patanjali calls it '*anitya suchi dukha nätma sunichya suchi sukätma*' meaning, the body is unclean and filled with misery but to consider the body to be our soul which is clean, eternal and blissful is the first klesha or disturbance. Such a misidentification is called avidya. This is a very important principle because most of our habits and attempts to obtain pleasure are directed through the body and its senses. Anything that comes out of this body—be it tears, sweat, mucus, blood, urine, stool—all are unclean. Being attached to the body and thinking that one is this body causes great disturbance.

SMITHA—FALSE EGO

Smitha means false ego. Ignorance evolves into false ego or false identification. The soul starts identifying at different levels with great absorption. Smitha means identifying very specifically with great emotions. When one starts doing so, one identifies oneself with such external expressions and becomes vulnerable to being easily affected by externalities. A case in point is our addiction to social media in recent years.

ÇUKHANUCAI RAGA—ATTACHMENT FOLLOWED BY MEMORIES

Raga is hankering or craving for pleasure. To attain that pleasure, one tries to remember past experiences and Patanjali refers to that as *sukhanucai raga*. Habits are formed by remembering the last experience of pleasure. This ability to summon past memories to create present experiences of pleasure leads to the development of attachment. As a result of attachment, memory promises that the same pleasure will be derived if one repeats the behaviour. This way, one gets trapped by memory preceding attachment which lies latent within the consciousness.

DVESHA—AVERSION/AVOIDING PAIN

Raga or attachments to past memories not only delivers pleasure but also pain. Such is the duality of this material world. Dvesha means avoiding pain. One tries to avoid painful memories of the past by resorting to addictive patterns as a distraction from that pain. Last-minute exam terror, escaping from the childhood trauma of abuse by indulging in intoxicants, being engrossed in sports and entertainment, and addiction to video games are some examples of people turning away from healing their pain and even suppressing it. This aversion causes a great disturbance.

ABINIVESHA—FEAR OF DEATH

Patanjali states that a fear of death, abhinivesha, is found in all classes of people including the greatest scholars who have acquired a tremendous amount of knowledge. Even the accumulation of knowledge cannot guarantee them freedom from the influence of death or the fear of death. This fear lies deep within our consciousness.

TWENTY-EIGHT

United We Stand

Human Quality: Team Spirit

Rishabh was driving his car on the highway in the hilly terrain of Munnar in Kerala. Just as he was about to get to his destination in the hills, his car suddenly broke down. This was his first visit to Kerala. Born and raised in Indore, he was not familiar with the local language and the car breaking down left him in a state of anxiety.

Just then, he found a middle-aged man riding a bullock cart. Thankfully, the man understood some Hindi and English. Rishabh managed to communicate that he needed help.

'Well,' the man sighed, 'thanks to my bull, I can try.'

Rishabh heaved a sigh of relief and became hopeful.

The man unyoked the bull from the cart and tied it to the car. He then tapped the bull and urged it to move forward. It made a start but was moving at a snail's pace.

Rishabh was happy to finally see the car move. He was looking forward to it reaching closer to his destination at the top of the hill.

'Ramu, Shyamu, Sudama, Hanuman,' the man cried. 'Come on, pull, pull, pull.'

The bull moved at a faster pace now, and so did the car, making Rishabh happier.

'Ramu, pull, Shyamu, pull, Sudama, pull, Hanuman, pull!' the man called out again.

The bull got faster. For Rishabh it was like witnessing magic as his car was making its way towards the top of the hills. He was curious to know who Ramu, Shyamu, Sudama and Hanuman were. However, he didn't want to interrupt the action. So he kept quiet and followed the car.

Finally, the car reached the top of the hill, and they parked it near a mechanic shop. Rishabh thanked the man profusely and made a donation for the bull. The man was thankful for the same. He was about to take his bull back when Rishabh asked him, 'May I know what were those names you were calling out?'

'Do you mean Ramu, Shyamu, Sudama and Hanuman?'

'Yes, exactly. Why were you saying that?'

The man smiled back.

'I'm very grateful,' Rishabh continued, 'that you helped me. And I am curious to know why you called out these names and how the bull gathered speed specifically after you called them out.'

'So,' the man began, 'the bull's name is Hanuman and he is quite old now. Over the last few months, he has turned blind too. To make sure he gets the inspiration and confidence, I started shouting the names of his associates in the farm— Ramu, Shyamu and Sudama.'

Rishabh was amazed by this thought process.

'Hanuman now felt that there were three other bulls by his side and that he was part of a team. He didn't feel alone.'

'Wow! This is brilliant.'

'And just hearing me and thinking he was part of a powerful team gave him the inspiration and the strength to do his best and move forward,' the man concluded.

How often have we experienced this in life? As they say, unity is strength. United we stand, divided we fall. This is a very important concept for us to understand as ultimately, we are social animals. We gain strength through our association with others.

In the *Srimad Bhagavatam* (1.10.11), it is described:

> sat-sangān mukta-duḥsaṅgo
> hātuṁ notsahate budhaḥ
> kīrtyamānaṁ yaśo yasya
> sakṛd ākarṇya rocanam

With the association of like-minded, positive people (mukta-duḥsaṅgo), we can become free from the influence of negativity. Overcoming weakness and challenging circumstances is difficult for a person individually. But when we know we have the association of other like-minded souls who want to be freed from the influence of ignorance, it is an inspiring factor which keeps us moving forward with great enthusiasm.'

Team spirit needs to be cultivated and nurtured, its blossoming is an ongoing process. The three steps to improving team spirit are:

Step 1: Connect with the greater purpose

It starts with purpose as that is the foundation of why we do what we do. Further, it helps instill a sense of belongingness and emotional connect. In the long run, it is important to rally people around a common thread, and that common thread is purpose. As professionals, we should help people in our teams find greater meaning in their daily tasks by conveying and communicating the purpose of our efforts clearly.

Step 2: Be emotionally engaged

When we are emotionally connected to a purpose, our subconscious mind pushes us to achieve our objective with much more vigour and gusto. We are driven towards the purpose as that becomes our guiding light. Further, when we encounter challenges in that pursuit, this emotional connect that we forge helps us recover and build resilience within.

Step 3: Create a culture of collaboration

In a cooperative culture we provide support only when asked. In a collaborative culture, we are proactive in offering assistance to other team members. Because we are emotionally connected, we find the drive to take initiative and work with people from within. Even when there are interpersonal challenges in a team, we are willing to look beyond small differences to work towards a higher goal.

TWENTY-NINE

Who's the Master?

Human Quality: Controlling the Mind

Once Sripada Sankaracharya was walking through the marketplace with his disciples. They saw a man dragging a cow by a rope.

Smiling, the acharya approached the man, told him to wait and asked the disciples to surround the scene.

'I am going to teach you something,' he announced. 'Tell me who is bound to whom?'

'Sorry?' the disciples wondered.

'Is the cow bound to this man' the acharya added, 'or is the man bound to the cow?'

The disciples said without hesitation: 'Of course the cow is bound to the man!' The acharya smiled.

'The man is the master,' added one disciple. 'He is holding the rope.'

Another disciple continued, 'The cow has to follow him wherever he goes. The man is the master and the cow is the slave.'

'Now watch this,' said the acharya, taking a pair of scissors from his bag.

The disciples were aware of their guru's greatness and waited with great anticipation to watch what was going to be revealed.

Within seconds, Sripada Sankaracharya cut the rope with the scissors. As soon as he did that, the cow ran away from the master. Baffled and desperate, the man ran after his cow instantly.

This was an aha moment for the disciples there.

'Look what is happening!' said the acharya. 'Do you see who the master is?'

Having learnt a deep lesson, the students nodded in disbelief.

'The cow is not at all interested in this man,' the acharya affirmed. 'The cow in fact, is trying to escape this man.'

The disciples folded their hands, prostrated at the lotus feet of their guru and thanked him for such a deep lesson from this simple incident. They walked along and Sripada Sankaracharya enlightened the students on controlling the mind.

In the Bhagavad Gita (6.5), it is stated:

uddhared ātmanātmānaṁ
nātmānam avasādayet
ātmaiva hy ātmano bandhur
ātmaiva ripur ātmanaḥ

One must deliver himself with the help of his mind and not degrade himself. The mind is the friend of the conditioned soul and his enemy as well.

Our mind, like the cow's, is not interested in the unwanted talks and vain acts we engage in. Although we input them in due to our conditioning, the mind is not at all interested in holding on to them. The moment we lose interest in all the garbage poured into our head and the moment we understand its futility, it will begin to disappear. Like the cow, it will escape and disappear.

Controlling our mind is important to ensure we are in firm control of our life. In another verse in the Gita, Lord Krishna asserts: 'For him who has conquered the mind, the mind is the best of friends; but for one who has failed to do so, his very mind will be the greatest enemy.'

1. **The mind is a tormentor, not a mentor**

    As we begin the journey of controlling our mind, we should first understand that the mind is an enemy. It's currently not in our control, rather it is controlling us with its diktats of material desires. Fundamentally, because we are souls, our position is *änandamäyä*. Änandamäyä means always blissful. Because we are part and parcel of God, and God is blissful, all-good, sat-cit-änanda, we are too. Sat means eternal, cit means full of knowledge and änanda means full of bliss. We are qualitatively the same but quantitatively infinitesimal.

    The soul is pleasure-seeking, but due to its identification with matter, and using the tool of the subtle body—mind, intelligence and false ego—it seeks pleasure in material objects. However, material objects have limitations and cannot satisfy the levels of pleasure sought by the soul via the mind. When unfulfilled, the mind torments us as it seeks higher degree of pleasure, unaware that it's searching in the wrong place. Pleasure in material objects is like a mirage in the desert. It appears to be there but it's not there.

2. **The mind may replay but we don't have to play along**

   Continuing the torment, the mind will replay its wants and keep pushing us further. Beware, that is a conundrum we shouldn't lend our ears to. Rather, we should focus our efforts on building robust spiritual understanding. When we do that, we channelize our energy in such a way that we educate our minds with the correct understanding and also clarify and work towards removing the fallacies subtly.

3. **The mind is like a dog that barks but can't bite unless we let it**

   This analogy should help us understand the loud noise that reverberates within us whenever we are in an agitated or excited state. It's the mind that 'barks' to grab our attention and calls out for the fulfilment of insatiable desires. We have a choice and fully developed free will as to whether we want to let it bite us or to stay away and ignore it.

   My spiritual master, Radhanath Swami, often speaks of a similar analogy. He says, 'Within every heart dwell two dogs, a bad dog and a good dog, both are at battle with one another. The bad dog represents our debased tendencies of envy, anger, lust, greed, arrogance and illusion. The good dog, our divine nature, is represented by forgiveness, compassion, self-control, generosity, humility and wisdom. Whichever dog we feed the most, through the choices we make and how we utilize our time, is empowered to bark the loudest and conquer the other. Virtue is to starve the bad dog and feed the good dog.'

4. **When the mind cries wolf know that it is the worst wolf**
    There is a well-known remark made by John Milton. He said, 'The mind is its own place and, in itself can make a heaven of hell and a hell of heaven.' Even for a minor discomfort or when life unsettles us slightly, the mind has the tendency to make noise inside and make us believe we are under attack. This has the potential to provoke us. Such a cry from the mind is based on past experiences and impressions (or *vasanas*), and the onus is on us to move forward without getting stuck in the past.

5. **Meditation minimizes inner friction and maximizes outer contribution**
    Meditation is a powerful way to minimize the friction inside. It calms the mind and can normalize its agitated state. In a normalized state, the mind becomes less volatile and more receptive. For us to take charge of the mind, besides meditation, we should also feed the intelligence with spiritual knowledge. Then, with able understanding, the intelligence can supersede the false ego, take charge and guide the mind in the right direction.

    Radhanath Swami reveals in his talks that all sacred scriptures and cultures caution us to not succumb to the mind's short-sighted urges for instant pleasure or relief. This demand for immediate pleasure is sought by giving in to negative forces within us and is akin to feeding the bad dog. The mind proposes its thoughts, desires and emotions so subtly and irresistibly that we unthinkingly consider them to be our own and indiscriminately act on them. Quoting the Bhagavad Gita, Radhanath Swami explains that the best way to deal with the mind is to treat it as a person different from ourselves. We need to critically examine its ideas, which are often detrimental to our long-term self-interest, just as we would examine the ideas expressed by someone else

THIRTY

The Most Important Part of the Body

Human Quality: Service

'My mother used to ask me what the most important part of the body is,' Riya began on the weekly podcast she recorded for a private firm. 'Through the years I took a guess at what I thought was the correct answer . . .'

Riya, a deeply spiritual and philosophical person, was intrigued by the human form of life—the power of the sixth sense and the unique ability of human beings to transform life and the world we live in like never before. A well-read person, she delved into the contents of various religious texts and always found their essence to present inspiring stories to her listeners. To make the listening worthwhile, she interspersed her philosophical learnings with engaging anecdotes from her life and stories from the books she read.

'When I was young,' she continued on her podcast, 'I thought sound was very important to us as humans, so I said, "My ears, Mommy."

'She replied, "No, but unfortunately, many people in the world we live in are deaf. Anyway, keep thinking about it and I will ask you again soon."

'A few weeks passed before she asked me again. Since making my first attempt, I had contemplated on another answer.

'So, this time I told her, "Mommy, sight is very important, so it must be our eyes."

'She looked at me and told me, "You are learning fast, but the answer is not correct because there are many people who are blind."

'Stumped again, I continued my quest for knowledge and over the years, she asked me a couple more times and always her answer was, "No. But you are getting smarter every year, my child."

'A year went by and my grandfather passed away. We were shocked as he was hale and hearty and he had no trace of any disease. A sudden heart attack took him away from us. We all sobbed that day, all day, literally. My father, who was supposed to be mentally strong, didn't control his emotions and shed many tears with us. I remember that especially because it was only the second time I saw him cry.

'As my grandfather's body was about to be taken away and as we bid him one final goodbye, my mother approached me and asked in a low tone, "Do you know the most important body part yet, my dear?"

'This was certainly not the moment to think about such a question and I was taken aback for a moment. I always thought of this as a game between her and me.

'She saw the confusion on my face and told me, "This question is very important. It shows that you have really lived in your life. For every body part you gave me in the past, I have told you were wrong, and I have given you an example why. But today is the day you need to learn this important lesson."

'She looked down at me as only a mother can. I saw her eyes well up with tears. She said, "My dear, the most important body part is the shoulder."

'Curious, I asked her, "Is it because it holds up my head?"

'She replied, "No, it is because it can hold the head of a friend or a loved one when they cry. Everybody needs a shoulder to cry on in life, my dear. Especially in times like these, as we are going through now."

'I could genuinely feel the gravity of her words as I was going through the same range of emotions then. So saying, my mother let her head rest on my shoulders as she bid a final goodbye to her father.

'Folks, what I want to leave you with today on this podcast is this: Let us cultivate more friendships, and create a positive difference in as many number of lives as possible. Let us find more shoulders to find comfort in and also provide ours to more people when they are in need.

'Nothing is as comforting as a shoulder, I conclude for today. Have a great weekend each one you.'

In the *Srimad Bhagavatam* (10.22.35), it is said:

etāvaj janma-sāphalyaṁ
dehinām iha dehiṣu
prāṇair arthair dhiyā vācā
śreya-ācaraṇaṁ sadā

It is the duty of every living being to perform welfare activities for the benefit of others with his life, wealth, intelligence and words. So let us utilize this life by acting for the benefit of others.

Since time immemorial, due to our contact with matter, we have been conditioned to have a doer mentality. For instance, if we give something in charity, we tend to think that it's because of our contribution that a certain activity is happening at the receiver's end. The true understanding of this situation is to see Krishna as the source of all wealth that exists. Out of His mercy, He has entrusted a minuscule portion of His wealth upon us temporarily. We are not owners but mere trustees of that minuscule portion of wealth for a limited time and it's our duty to use that wealth in a way that pleases the owner, Shri Krishna. We act as mere servants of the Supreme Lord and that's our true position as part and parcel of God.

Servant leadership is a leadership style that prioritizes the growth, well-being and empowerment of employees. It aims to foster an inclusive environment that enables everyone in the organization to thrive as their authentic self. Whereas traditional leadership focuses on the success of the company or organization, servant leadership puts employees first to grow the organization through their commitment and engagement. When implemented correctly, servant leadership can help foster trust, accountability, growth and inclusion in the workplace.

The theory of servant leadership was advanced by Robert K. Greenleaf, who popularized the term in a 1970s essay titled 'The Servant as Leader.' After reading the book *Journey to the East*, Greenleaf was inspired by the main character, Leo, a servant who disappears from work. After his disappearance, the productivity and effectiveness of the rest of the workers falls apart, revealing that Leo was, in fact, a leader all along. This led Greenleaf to believe that servant leadership is effective in its ability to allow workers to relate to leaders and vice versa, creating more trust and autonomy for workers. Greenleaf first put this theory to test while working as an executive at AT&T, and it's gained traction over the years as an effective leadership style.

Greenleaf initially proposed an 'I serve' mentality for servant leadership and based it on the two main premises of 'I serve because I am the leader' and 'I am the leader because I serve'. The first premise is focused on altruism, a selfless concern for others, while the second premise hinges on a person's ambition to become a leader.

The following are the nine important traits of a servant leader. A servant leader:

1. Is a servant first
2. Makes sure that other peoples' highest priority needs are served
3. States vision or goal first
4. Actively listens to others
5. Speaks the truth
6. Is trustworthy
7. Assists others in their development
8. Cares for the well-being of all people
9. Sustains the hope that both the organization and its people will reach their desired future

THIRTY-ONE

Prayers for Prasadam

Human Quality: Patience

In the temple town of Srirangam, there was once a man named
Bhaskar who would visit the temple daily to get the prasadam,
which was distributed freely to all. Although many devotees
thronged the temple for a darshan of Lord Ranganath and
were then offered the prasadam, he was different. He would
enter the temple premises just as the prasadam was being
distributed and further, he would often create a scene by
showing up with huge containers and ask for them to be filled
with prasadam. He would not request but demand it as he
needed to feed his seven family members.

When people questioned why he disturbed the ambience,
Bhaskar would respond, 'I want food for my six children.
They will go hungry if you do not give me the prasadam.'

If things escalated, he would sometimes shout and warn
people of severe consequences should his children die of
hunger. Fearing consequential curses, the authorities would
oblige and let him be served first to ease the atmosphere.
One temple worker decided to discuss the matter with

Sripada Ramanujacharya. After the acharya was apprised of the situation, he decided to take up the matter himself.

The next morning, when Bhaskar arrived again, he caused a big disturbance. Sripada Ramanujacharya walked out of the premises to meet him. Devotees who were arguing with Bhaskar became silent when they saw the acharya approach the scene. However, Bhaskar continued, although in a feebler voice.

The acharya walked to him and asked, 'Why are you making so much hue and cry here?'

'Well, I have six children in my house,' Bhaskar replied. 'I must feed them. Therefore, I cannot stand in the line behind everybody because I am anxious.'

'But why are you anxious?' the acharya asked.

'I don't know . . .' he started off in a high pitch and then gradually lowered his volume, 'whether in the end I will get it or not. So, I have to be right at the beginning and therefore I pushed myself to get to the front. That way, I'm assured of a good quantity food to feed my wife and six children.'

'Do you know the "Vishnu Sahasranamam"?'

'I'm not very advanced,' he replied in a polite tone out of respect for the acharya. 'I only know the first few verses.'

There was pin-drop silence as all devotees who had assembled observed the acharya transforming the man. The prasadam distribution was paused as the volunteers too were focusing on the actions of the acharya.

'Can you chant?' the acharya asked politely.

'Sure,' he began, '*viśvaṁ viṣṇurvaṣaṭkārō bhūta bhavya bhavatprabhuḥ bhūtakṛdbhūtabhṛdbhāvō bhūtātmā bhūtabhāvanaḥ.*'

Then, Bhaskar paused and tried to recall the verses but he couldn't recite more without referring to the text.

'That's all right,' the Acharya said. 'So, you know only six out of the thousand names of Lord Vishnu?'

'Yes, Swamiji. I know only this much.'

In deep thought, the acharya advised, 'Can you just focus on the sixth name, which is Bhutabhrt?'

'Yes, of course.'

'Bhutabhrt means one who nourishes the entire universe. I request you to everyday chant with faith, great feeling and emotion, bhutabhrte namah. When you do that, you offer obeisance to the Supreme nourisher of the universe.'

'Definitely, Swamiji,' he assured. 'I'll do that.'

The acharya concluded, If you chant this mantra fervently 108 times a day, Lord Ranganath will personally come and deliver this prasadam to you; have faith.'

Bhaskar offered prostrated obeisance to Sripada Ramanujacharya as he walked into the temple. He then collected prasadam in the containers and left for home. A week passed. Prasadam began to be served smoothly. The commotion that used to be prevalent outside the temple premises was no longer there as Bhaskar never came for prasadam collection.

One evening, the priest approached the acharya and said, 'We are seeing a bewildering phenomenon. Daily, we offer profuse quantities of *bhoga* (food) to the Lord but when we open the container later to take back the offered prasadam, a substantial part is missing.'

The acharya listened to this intently in deep meditation. He remained silent.

'Now,' the priest added, 'Bhaskar, who used to come and fight with us for taking more prasadam no longer visits the temple. So, we are in doubt whether he's the one who is mysteriously stealing the prasadam.'

'Oh really?' Ramanujacharya asked. 'So, you mean to say that the prasadam goes missing after it is offered?'

Later that evening, Sripada Ramanuja crossed the Kollidam River and walked up to Bhaskar's hut. As soon he saw the former approaching his hut, Bhaskar came out running and offered obeisance to the acharya.

'Oh, my dear Gurudev,' Bhaskar said respectfully, 'by your grace and blessings, the hunger problem in our house is solved.'

'How did that happen?' the acharya inquired.

'From the time you instructed me to chant "Bhutabhrte namah" 108 times, a young boy from temple comes home daily with abundant quantity of prasadam. So much so that even after our entire family is satisfied, we have some left over. We then distribute it to people nearby.'

'A young boy?' the acharya confirmed. 'How did he begin visiting you?'

'Well,' Bhaskar responded, 'I thought you have instructed this boy to deliver the prasadam. Whenever I have asked him for his name, he says, "I am a disciple of Ramanuja." Therefore, I assumed that you are the one who is sending this boy.'

Sripada Ramanujacharya meditated for a moment and realized through his divine power that the boy was Shri Ranganath Swami Himself who was dropping by Bhaskar's hut and mysteriously facilitating the needs of His devotee. The acharya wished Bhaskar well, blessed him and took his leave.

In the Bhagavad Gita (9.5), it is said:

na ca mat-sthāni bhūtāni
paśya me yogam aiśvaram
bhūta-bhṛn na ca bhūta-stho
mamātmā bhūta-bhāvanaḥ

Here, Krishna tells Arjuna to not be surprised by the beauty of His mystic power. He goes on to say that He is indeed the nourisher of the entire universe. Simply by His supreme will, everything is created, everything is sustained, everything is maintained and everything is annihilated. There is no difference between His mind and Himself (as there is a difference between us and our present material mind) because He is absolute spirit.

In the above story, the first exchange between Sripada Ramanujacharya and Bhaskar is of significance. In that conversation, the seeds of *Hari bhakti*, worship were sown by the acharya in the heart of the latter. The spiritual power of the acharya played a role in transforming Bhaskar. In life, we should always seek association with exalted souls (acharyas) as they can show us mercy and elevate us. But, for that, we should be open-minded, receptive, sincere in practice and have a learning mindset. On his part, Bhaskar was obedient and attached deep importance to the words of the acharya.

Interestingly, he knew only six out of the thousand holy names of Lord Vishnu. Mathematically, that's a meagre 0.6 per cent, yet he focused on the one name that the acharya had instructed him to chant. What we learn from this is that spiritual knowledge matters but it's not the be all and end all.

Even if we have limited knowledge, we should have faith in the words of the gurus and acharyas who come from a line of disciples of the Supreme Lord to translate that knowledge into service unto His lotus feet. When we do that, He reciprocates. Patience is a virtue and it is required to deepen faith. The Lord is not one to pander to the immediate needs of people. We live in a world where 'instant' has become the norm—hyperlocal e-commerce, fast foods, instant coffee, etc. However, faith needed for spiritual progress calls for patience.

Here are five tips to improve patience:

1. **Stop resisting and respond rather than react**

   In the above story, Bhaskar could have questioned the instruction of the acharya and resisted it. However, he didn't react but responded in the affirmative. The mind tends to assume supremacy over the words of others with its 'know-it-all' mindset. It's very important for us to assess situations on a case-to-case basis and respond accordingly. This is a first step to cultivating patience.

2. **Meditate on the effects of impatience**

   Another way is to look at the flip side. That is, in the event we display impatience, what could be the possible consequences? How that would worsen a given situation or disturb relationships? People typically learn from the mistakes they have committed. That said, real learning happens when we don't repeat previously committed mistakes.

3. **Look for the positive possibilities in the negative**

   When we are put through challenging situations, we tend to get swayed by the apparent negativity and think that all is down and out. The best prayer to God in such times is to seek strength to face the challenging situation. When we are put through such situations and we face them with humility, we build resilience. This helps build mental muscle and resolve without falling prey to pessimism.

4. **Utilize time to show gratitude**

    Faith can be deepened by being grateful to God for the many gifts that He has bestowed on us. It can start with the basics that we take for granted: an able body, well-performing sensory organs, the intelligence to discriminate between good and bad, loving parents and a caring family among others. By displaying gratitude, the heart becomes a more fertile home for virtues such as patience, tolerance, etc.

5. **Befriend the situation**

    Based on the law of karma, we go through situations that give us pain. As they say, 'Pain is compulsory, suffering is optional'. That said, God has provided each one of us (in the human form of life) fully developed free will. We can make a certain choice to respond to situations in life. So, we have an opportunity to embrace the situation we are in, befriend it and see through a lens that lets us discover aspects to help us learn, develop and grow. That way, we remain positive and see God's invisible hand in every situation in life. We see how He has implanted challenging situations in our lives to aid our learning and thereby promote our spiritual progress.

THIRTY-TWO

The Power of Tolerance

Human Quality: Tolerance

A saintly person was once passing through a village. That village was known for its sinful people, and they were indeed infamous for insulting others.

As the saint passed through, they caught hold of him and started blaspheming him, defaming him and shouting expletives at him. The saintly person that he was, he stood there unfazed, hearing all of it quietly.

When they finally ended, he looked at them and said politely, 'I'm in a hurry. I need to go to another town. When I return here on the way back, you can continue with it.'

The villagers were flabbergasted. They looked at him and said, 'We hurled so many insults at you and you did not get affected? How is it possible?'

The saint replied calmly, 'Well, maybe ten years ago, I may have been affected by this.'

'What about now?' asked one villager.

'Since then, I engage in chanting of God's holy names, I meditate and I am engaged in self-realization. I realize that my identity will not change due to one incident.'

The people marvelled at him. They wondered if such people could still exist in the world.

The sage continued, 'I don't accept what you give me. You shouted all kinds of abuses at me. But I didn't accept any of them. I am not allowing you to hurt me. Further, you can only affect me if I accept those abuses and the ill feelings which you've thrown at me.'

The people felt ashamed. And at the same time, they developed deep respect for the most sagacious gentleman they had ever met in their life.

'I try to control myself,' the sage added. 'I try to control my mind. A person with a controlled mind will not allow anything, as far as circumstances are concerned, to affect him and impact him.'

The mood of the crowd changed, and the seer observed that they were listening to him in rapt attention. Hence he wanted to conclude with an analogy that could pierce their hearts and transform them deeply.

'Think of it this way,' he began, 'a flaming branch of a tree may be hurled but if that flaming branch comes in contact with a river, it gets extinguished and becomes a flowing log in that river.'

This light of knowledge from the saint illuminated the ignorance in the minds of the people.

'Therefore, all the abuses that you threw at me were like a flaming torch. But my mind, like a cold, flowing river, extinguished them,' he concluded

The villages begged forgiveness and prostrated in front of the seer as he moved along.

The *Srimad Bhagavatam* (1.18.48) describes:

> *tiraskṛtā vipralabdhāḥ*
> *śaptāḥ kṣiptā hatā api*
> *nāsya tat pratikurvanti*
> *tad-bhaktāḥ prabhavo 'pi hi*

If one is insulted, if one is cheated, if one is cursed, if one is neglected, if one is killed, in spite of all of these, great personalities are extremely tolerant in all situations and they do not counter. They learn how to tolerate this because they know that the power of tolerance is the pathway to holistic progress in life.

Fundamentally, great personalities understand that they are not the body but the soul. As a result, they understand that what is being hurled at them is aimed at the body and not the soul. Even if killed, what is killed is the body and not the soul.

The world we live in is filled with conflicts. Right through our life, at different points of time, we are put in situations that can lead to conflict. Conflicts can be resolved by improving and increasing one's tolerance.

Let's discuss a few practices we can inculcate to develop tolerance:

1. **Practise bearing insult and dishonour from others**
   When people hurl insults or abuses at us, it's an expression of their intolerance stemming from their inability to control their mind. Should we also respond in that fashion, then ours will be a similar story too. If we

get provoked, it subtly indicates that we admit the truth in their abuse. If we possess self-confidence, we are not taken aback by the words of others. It can seem difficult to internalize such levels of self-confidence, but it's doable with sound philosophical understanding and consistent practice of spirituality.

2. **Cultivate deeper understanding of the material world**
   In the Bhagavad Gita, Shri Krishna says, *duùkhälayam açäçvatam*, meaning that the material world is temporary and is full of miseries. The miseries can come in the form of embarrassing or even irritating situations, and unless one is inclined to be very forgiving, they will become infected by a vindictive mentality. Such a mentality, if unchecked, can disturb peace in the mind and further pollute it too.

3. **Tolerate provoking situations**
   Srila Prabhupada, the founder acharya of ISKCON, used to often say that the greatness of a person is defined by their ability to tolerate provoking situations. Bringing one's mind under control is easier in normal circumstances than during provoking situations. That's because when we are provoked, one's mind gets agitated and hence we tend to lose control of our mind. Gaining control over the mind is facilitated by performing yoga, meditation and by chanting of the holy names of the Lord, like the Hare Krishna *maha mantra*. Performing such activities positively energizes the mind and provides stability to it. As a result, even if provoked, the mind holds up and doesn't get swayed by external influence easily.

THIRTY-THREE

The Ninety-Nine Club

Human Quality: Greed

Vinod Sampat was the king of a large Dravidian kingdom headquartered in Kanchipuram. State tax revenues filled up the treasury but despite all the wealth, King Vinod was never really happy. The behaviour of one of his personal servants, Sparsh, always intrigued Vinod. Although earning a meagre salary, Sparsh was always blissful. The king was keen to learn the secret behind this poor man's happiness.

Returning to the palace after a rather stressful revenue trip one afternoon, the king saw Sparsh after a break. Sparsh was busy organizing a few things for his master's return, but at the same time he was smiling and looked cheerful.

'I wish I can be in a state of happiness like Sparsh,' thought the worn-out king.

'Jai,' he called out for one of his ministers and asked, 'Sparsh is always cheerful. He has such an uplifting effect on me. How can I attain such a state of deep happiness?'

'Your Majesty,' the wise minister replied, 'Sparsh is not a member of the Ninety-Nine Club yet.'

Puzzled, the king asked, 'Ninety-Nine Club? What is that?'

The minister smiled and requested, 'Please give me a few weeks' time and allow me to demonstrate what I mean.'

Meanwhile, Jai placed a bag of ninety-nine gold coins at a spot right inside Sparsh's room. In a few hours' time, as expected by Jai, Sparsh picked up the bag. He opened the bag and upon looking inside, his eyes glittered like gold.

'Who could this belong to?' he asked himself, 'So many guests come here every day and many leave us tips. But this is the first time someone has left me a fortune!'

Fearful at the same time, he ducked the bag under his belt and went to use the washroom. Thrilled and impatient, he began counting the coins. His joy oozed up exponentially at every coin. Approaching the nineties, his feet tapped as he anticipated a jackpot of hundred solid gold nuggets.

'Ninety-nine,' and there it stopped.

'I must have miscounted,' muttered a confused Sparsh.

'Breathe easy and count slowly this time,' he told himself.

He counted twice and the number didn't go beyond ninety-nine.

He counted one last time. With the same outcome, a nervous thought arose in him, 'It must have been a hundred coins obviously. I must have dropped a coin rushing to the toilet.'

He walked back to the room and he couldn't find it. He frantically checked a few times under the sofa chairs, then behind the curtains and then beside the numerous flower vases. Even that did not help him locate that elusive hundredth gold coin.

Sparsh's destiny had showered upon him gold but the missing hundredth coin tainted his joy. Eclipsed by restlessness and anxiety, Sparsh skipped lunch as his eyes kept searching for the elusive coin while his mind kept wandering.

'O Varadharaja Swami,' he prayed to the deity of Kanchipuram, 'you have given me so much even when I have not asked for it; now, all I ask is for one coin. That will be it!'

A day passed. Pensive, Sparsh thought to himself, 'Maybe there is a message in this for me? Maybe Lord Varadharaja wants me to earn that hundredth gold coin.'

He was convinced.

'Yes,' he cheered himself. 'I must work hard, save and then buy that hundredth coin.'

He further comforted himself, saying, 'Of course I've heard that God takes a hundred steps towards you when you take one step towards Him. Perhaps in my case the Lord has taken ninety-nine steps and now He expects me to complete the loop of a hundred. Yes, yes, it's all making sense now.'

A perfectly achievable target. It will do me a world of good and bring me a sense of achievement, confidence and fulfilment.' In this way Sparsh validated his greed without actually feeling grateful to God.

Possessed now, Sparsh wallowed in a newly dug pond of yearning for more earnings. 'Since this is blessed money I shall not spend it. I will not tell my wife about it, she always has a long laundry list of unwanted things. She will spend my fortune on silk and sandals. Rather, I will bury this bag under my bed and once I earn one more coin, I will put a deposit of my hundred gold coins at the bank and start earning interest. With that I will build a new house. A house with one, no, two floors. I will then earn rent and I will use the rental income to invest in land and employ farmers to harvest for me.' Sparsh's greed divorced him from the very purpose of earning money, which was the sustenance and happiness of his family.

Driven to purchase a gold coin, Sparsh began working very hard, taking up extra responsibilities at the palace, working late hours in the evenings and spending the weekends working at the palace kitchen. Always considering his endeavours insufficient, he became edgy and tired. Due to lack of enough rest, he became short-tempered. Over time, he became irritable and would often shout at his wife. This disturbed a harmonious marital relationship.

A few weeks passed and Jai, the wise minister, approached King Vinoth Sampat, 'My lord, do you remember our previous discussion on Sparsh?'

'Yes, of course,' the king nodded. 'I do.'

'Can you observe any change in him right now?'

'Oh yes!' the king beamed, 'In fact, I wanted to let you know last week. Why has he become irritable lately? That equipoise is missing. In fact, I have gathered feedback that he has had many nasty exchanges with other servants in the palace.'

'That's because, your Highness,' Jai beamed, 'he has now formally joined the Ninety-Nine Club.'

In the Bhagavad Gita (16.11), Lord Krishna says:

> *cintām aparimeyāṁ ca*
> *pralayāntām upāśritāḥ*
> *kāmopabhoga-paramā*
> *etāvad iti niścitāḥ*

Making unlimited plans to possess more and more can slowly cause the loss of stability of our mind. The invisible strings of unfulfilled desires pull the gracious gifts we have from right beneath our nose. Constant chasing of the proverbial carrot causes frequent burnout since the dream for more is paid in the currency of sleep. One-sided financial ambitions cause major imbalances in life, collapsing or damaging the foundation of deeper relationships.

At another point in the Bhagavad Gita, Krishna has conclusively labelled greed as one of the three gateways to a miserable life (lust and anger being the other two; it's worth observing the close bond the three of them share).

It is greed that gives rise to enmity, be it between individuals or between communities. While greed for possessions makes you desperate and foolhardy, greed for attention can leave you lonely, even if you are at the top.

What is the root of greed?

Lust, an unchecked desire for more. Unfulfilled lust creates anger in us and fulfilled lust creates greed. Someone's hunger and thirst can be satisfied by food and drink. Similarly, their anger can be satisfied by chastisement and disciplining. But a greedy person cannot be satisfied, even if they possess the entire world and enjoy everything in it.

What is the root of lust?

Selfishness, an overcompensated drive to enjoy, even at the expense of others, howsoever close they may be to us.

How can selfishness be pacified?

By experiencing a higher sense of fulfilment through service to God, with whom we share the actual closest relationship.

Just as a person wearing shoes on his feet can walk on pebbles and thorns without danger, a self-satisfied person finds happiness everywhere and is undeterred by the pebbles and thorns of the inevitable challenges of this world.

THIRTY-FOUR

Think of the Master Always!

Human Quality: Faith

It was a foggy morning in New Delhi. It was peak winter in early January and flights were delayed due to unfavourable weather conditions. The sun began emerging from the clouds slowly, and the sky cleared up around ten in the morning. The airport authorities signalled that it was time for flights to take off gradually but with caution.

A Jaipur-bound flight took off, and as it headed close to 500 feet above sea level, turbulent weather conditions re-emerged and the flight crew urged passengers to keep the seat belt on. Within a few minutes, the flight started shaking uncontrollably.

The pilot announced, 'Passengers are requested to fasten their seat belts and sit tight. We are going through turbulence.'

The passengers became more vigilant.

As the weather became more turbulent, a sense of commotion pervaded. The passengers became uneasy.

'Please be careful, anything can happen,' Rajiv, a middle-aged man warned a girl seated next to him. She was dressed in a red frock and must have been in her early teens. She remained as cool as a cucumber.

The man looked around to see his fellow passengers in a different state of mind altogether. Some were crying, some were praying with their eyes closed. Overall, a sense of panic gripped the flight.

In stark contrast was this girl with a smile on her face, as if nothing had gone wrong. Considering he was petrified as well, he didn't express his curiosity and continued with his prayers in angst. After close to twenty minutes of turbulence, finally the clouds cleared up and the flight went on with its trajectory without disturbance. All the passengers felt relieved, including Rajiv. There was an air of calmness in the flight.

Rajiv looked at the girl seated next to him, she remained as cool as she had been for the last few minutes.

Now, he couldn't resist and he began a conversation, 'Hey, what's your name?'

'Malati,' she replied.

'Malati,' he began, 'I am curious, in the middle of the turbulence, as everyone was freaking out, here you were totally calm and peaceful. How did you manage that?'

She smiled back, 'My father is the pilot. And I am confident that he will take me home safely.'

This confidence that the girl had in her father is what we must have in our Supreme Father, when we are faced with the storms of calamity, disparity, difficulty and challenges in our life.

In the *Hari Bhakti Vilas*, it is said:

ānukūlyasya saṅkalpaḥ
prātikūlyasya varjanam
rakṣiṣyatīti viśvāso
goptṛtve varaṇaṁ tathā
ātma-nikṣepa-kārpaṇye
ṣaḍ-vidhā śaraṇāgatiḥ

One of the symptoms of a surrendered devotee is rakñiñyatéti viçväso, he has full faith that the Lord will protect him. Therefore let us have that confidence in the Lord's protection and lead life with great confidence.

It is not an easy task to cultivate such deep faith. Added to this, we live in a world where people can develop addictions easily. Not just smoking and drinking but addiction to gadgets is rampant. It can be difficult for someone to recover from their addictive patterns. A motivating pep talk can be a starting point but it is insufficient.

Sage Patanjali writes, '*Yoga chitta gritty nirodh*', that yoga alone can solve the problem when one is stuck in unhealthy habits. Yoga is the bona fide treatment through which one can get out of this complex cycle of habits. The cycle of habits runs at full speed like an electric fan within our minds; yoga simply unplugs the connection and stops the electricity from flowing through. However, the fan doesn't stop instantly, it gradually slows down and after some time, it becomes still. The word 'nirodh' in his statement refers to this full stop. We can infer from here that yoga is not just different gymnastic postures. Yoga is the process of bringing the changing states of mind to stillness.

Srila Prabhupada, ISKCON's founder acharya, the one who revolutionized the spiritual movement in the West by turning several drug addicts and hippies in New York and San Francisco in the 1960s and 1970s into spiritual practitioners of bhakti, has formed a wonderful formula. It consists of the five Ds.

Following the five Ds diligently, one can cultivate good habits and develop deep faith in the Supreme Lord. That way, we can let go of *anarthas* or contaminations of this material world and purify the consciousness to become self-realized.

1. Discipline

Discipline in chanting the holy names of the Lord regularly. You may wonder why especially the discipline of chanting the holy names would relieve one from addictive behaviour and cultivate good habits.

The ancient text of *Srimad Bhagavatam* states:

śvādah pulkasao vāpi śuddhyeran yasya kīrtanāt

That even a dog-eater shall be purified from chanting of the holy names of Krishna. As we have seen before, to break this compulsive behaviour formed over a lifetime, we compel ourselves to form a new behaviour that counteracts all material impressions by planting the seeds of transcendence within our consciousness.

Lord Chaitanya Mahaprabhu's first words of the *siksastakam* were 'Ceto darpana marjanam'. Now, our *chitta* is affected by disturbances and different mental states that lead to impressions, and then to actions and finally reactions. Thie holy names simply cleanse that dirt in the mirror of our consciousness which is hiding us from perceiving the Absolute Truth.

2. Discrimination

We should cultivate the sense of discrimination: the ability to demarcate right from wrong, healthy from unhealthy, moral from immoral. For this, we need a bona fide guide. This guide as per the Vedic tradition is dispersed in three forms. Sadhu, sanga, shastra. A saintly person who has seen the truth, the association of people who have developed clarity in pursuing a higher purpose and then the revealed scriptures.

One such scripture, the Bhagavad Gita, advises that we counteract our material addiction with spiritual addiction.

The Bhagavad Gita (2.59) says,

viṣayā vinivartante
nirāhārasya dehinaḥ
rasa-varjaṁ raso 'py asya
paraṁ dṛṣṭvā nivartate

The embodied soul may be restricted from sense enjoyment, though the taste for sense objects remains. But ceasing such engagements by experiencing a higher taste, he is fixed in consciousness.

Krishna Katha can be so intoxicating and provide such a high sense of pleasure that it can beat the pleasures of lower degrees. By engaging one's senses in hearing and reading the scriptures, clarity is born and addiction is banished.

3. Detachment

Detachment from sense objects helps us control our senses from pursuing them for enjoyment. This way, the pattern is disrupted. However, the best way to practise detachment is by worshipping deities. To come to the level of understanding that we are not this body-mind, we also need to acknowledge that anything available in this material world is not for our enjoyment but for Krishna's.

By worshipping the deities of Krishna, we can gradually develop detachment. Because He becomes the centre of our lives, our needs and wants can become insignificant in front of His. By cooking and offering Him the best palatable dishes out of love and devotion, we become detached from enjoying sense objects. This way, by honouring the prasadam or remnants of the food tasted by the Lord, our tongue is controlled. By controlling the tongue, we conquer the urges of our belly and genitals, the main residences of lust. Once lust, the biggest enemy, is under control, detachment is achieved easily.

4. Determination

The fourth step towards overcoming addiction is becoming determined to break patterns. This determination can increase by serving the devotees of the Lord. As we serve the devotees of the Lord, we also simultaneously associate with the pure devotees. By pleasing them, we immediately feel blessed with purity of consciousness that increases *vairagya*, or determination, to renounce material attachments.

Overcoming the vast ocean of material impressions, *samsara sagara*, is not so easy. Unless we obtain the mercy of those who have already crossed it, we won't be able to swim across this seemingly never-ending ocean.

5. Dedication

The Bhagavad Gita (2.67) says,

> *indriyāṇāṁ hi caratāṁ*
> *yan mano 'nuvidhīyate*
> *tad asya harati prajñāṁ*
> *vāyur nāvam ivāmbhasi*

As a strong wind sweeps away a boat on the water, even one of the roaming senses on which the mind focuses can carry away a man's intelligence.

Increasing dedication by visiting holy places, we absorb the higher vibrations of the great souls who had served the Lord with great dedication in that very place thousands of years ago. The grace of all those devotees flow into our consciousness and this induces a sense of dedication.

To recap, let's recall the five Ds—Discipline, Discrimination, Detachment, Determination and Dedication—to get over bad habits and cultivate good habits, like instilling deep faith in God, Krishna.

THIRTY-FIVE

Quality Determines Success

Human Quality: Gratitude

In the beautiful city of Dispur, Assam, lived Deepankar Boro, a wealthy entrepreneur. A self-made man, after graduating in electrical engineering, he followed his heart, pursued his passion and entered the fashion industry. Driven by his aesthetic sense, he started a fashion brand that became a rage among the youth within no time. Thanks to the deep penetration of the internet and the wide distribution facilitated by e-commerce, his clothing brand reached the far and wide reaches of the country. Encouraged by the response and the adoration his fashion brand had, he was keen to expand to parts of South-east Asia, to start with. Indonesia, Singapore and Vietnam being the target countries. The quick success he gathered in his thirties made him show gratitude to God. While he strategized, worked hard and kept himself abreast of the latest trends in fashion, he acknowledged the invisible hand of God that guided him and steered his company to success in almost every initiative of theirs.

As a means of thanksgiving, whenever he was in town, he made it a practice to visit the Janaki Ballabh Mandir in town. Taking darshan of Shri Ram, Lakshman and Janaki Devi made him feel good and he felt connected to Their Lordships. As a result of this connectedness, he donated to the temple from his profits and contributed immensely to the social and spiritual activities pursued by the temple. Over time, Deepankar became a well-respected gentleman among the temple community. Although he was doing very well for himself professionally and married to a chaste woman, he was upset about one absence in his life. Although the couple was married for over ten years, they could never beget a child. Deepankar explored the best of treatments available globally, but this remained elusive. Of late, his prayers to Their Lordships focused on this one aspect and he sought their blessings for the same.

One early morning on a Sunday, as he was making his way out of the temple after darshan, he was accompanied by the temple priest. They discussed plans for the upcoming Ram Navami celebrations and how they could make the festivities grander this year. Just as Deepankar was about to step outside the temple complex, the priest stopped him. As Deepankar looked down, there lay a baby wrapped in a tattered cloth.

'Jai Shri Ram,' the priest called out.

Deepankar instinctively looked around to locate the parents of this baby. It was early morning and as it was a Sunday, the streets were deserted. Even the priest didn't know what to do about this. After deep thought, the priest suggested, 'Why don't you see this situation as a message from Lord Ram, take care of the child and look after his welfare?'

Although taken aback for a moment, he humbly accepted the suggestion of the priest and took the child home with him. His kind wife cooperated and agreed to look after the child. They named the child Sundar and admitted him to a boarding school under the auspicious care of a charitable trust. As years passed, Deepankar got him well educated in a management school and Sundar got employed in a multinational company in Kolkata. Deepankar turned sixty and his clothing brand became a name to reckon with across Asia. He won many global awards and became a well-known business magnate. Yet he remained a humble devotee of Lord Ram and continued to visit the temple every Sunday. He also made it a point to speak to Sundar over the phone once a week. Sundar had a lot of affection for Deepankar and his wife and remained grateful to what they had done for him.

As the years passed and Deepankar became less active in the business, he requested Sundar to relocate to Dispur and join the business. Sundar kindly agreed and joined the business in a managerial role. In the company, there was a coterie of middle management who were not too pleased with Sundar joining. They saw him as a threat to their growth, knowing well about his background and how he was under Deepankar's shelter. There was a sense of envy and discomfort that pervaded their minds. They wanted to find ways to create a rift between them or, at least, find faults in the newly joined manager.

They always had an eye on Sundar and became more observant of his activities. In a week's time, they sensed something fishy in his activities. They observed that every evening, Sundar would go to one corner of the office, open a locker, unlock a box within it, spend a few seconds there, close the box and then head out. After discussing this among themselves, they thought this could be an opportunity to show Sundar in a bad light and create acrimony between Deepankar and Sundar.

The coterie approached Deepankar the next day, 'Sir, sorry to bother you.'

'No problem at all,' said the kind leader who practised the art of active listening.

'We have come together to unravel something fishy happening at work,' said one of the leaders.

'Please tell me how I can help.'

'Sir, we suspect that Sundar, whom you have recently appointed as senior manager in the category management team is siphoning money.'

'What are you saying?' Deepankar exclaimed.

'Yes, sir. We have observed him do something fishy around the locker given to him on the ground floor. We should resolve this.'

'I doubt he does that, but I value your loyalty to the company and I am more than happy to step in and resolve the issue.'

'Thank you, sir.'

'Considering I appointed him here, it's my duty to steer clear of any integrity issue, both for me and my referrals.'

Right away, Deepankar walked up to Sundar's cabin with the coterie of leaders and spoke about what bothered them about his behaviour.

Although initially hesitant, Sundar recognized the integrity concerns looming large and agreed to address them. They walked up to the locker.

Yet again, Sundar felt hesitant now to unlock the box.

'Please open this box,' said one of the leaders. 'We want to look within. This is suspicious.'

Sundar unlocked it, and to every one's surprise, there was an old, tattered cloth. The coterie was both puzzled and apologetic. In a few seconds, Deepankar's eyes became moist. Only Sundar and Deepankar could recognize what it was.

'What is this?' asked one of the leaders in a low tone, reflecting politeness.

'This reflects my humble beginnings,' said an emotional Sundar. 'The times have changed, and I have come a long way as a person.'

The leaders looked at each other in surprise and also a sense of guilt.

Deepankar looked at Sundar proudly.

'But I'll be ungrateful,' continued Sundar, looking at Deepankar, 'if I don't, time and again, remind myself of where my journey began and thank the people who have made me who I am today.'

The foundation of success is gratitude, followed by humility and a service attitude. Without the foundation of gratitude, one cannot be humble and display a service attitude.

In the *Srimad Bhagavatam* (7.9.28), it is said:

> *evaṁ janaṁ nipatitaṁ prabhavāhi-kūpe*
> *kāmābhikāmam anu yaḥ prapatan prasaṅgāt*
> *kṛtvātmasāt surarṣiṇā bhagavan gṛhītaḥ*
> *so 'haṁ kathaṁ nu visṛje tava bhṛtya-sevām*

Here, Prahalada Maharaja, while offering prayers to Lord Narasimhadeva says, 'My dear Lord, on this occasion, when I have received your grace, I'm simply remembering my spiritual teacher, Sripada Narada *muni*, by whose grace I got the opportunity to change the direction of my life, was prevented from falling into hellish conditions and now I have the opportunity to see you and serve you. At this moment, I only aspire to somehow or the other serve Srila Narada muni in any insignificant manner so that I can repay my debt towards him.'

My spiritual master, His Holiness Radhanath Swami, emphasizes very often on this very important virtue—gratitude. Let me share some of my learnings from his teachings.

Gratitude is a divine virtue that is so important that other divine virtues cannot exist without it. Spirituality grows like seeds within our heart. The goodness of our lifestyle protects that seed. Our spiritual practice of chanting God's names, reading scriptures, doing *seva* (service) for God and others waters that seed. But gratitude is what makes the ground fertile so that all these other virtues can have their maximum effect. A fertile soil allows the seed to have deep roots and grow very strong, and for that a grateful heart is essential.

Gratitude is to see beyond the immediate circumstances that come upon us and to seek the essence of that situation, that is real wisdom. We need to see every situation as a beautiful opportunity to grow if we are to be grateful. All the dualities in life, success or failure, honour and dishonour, are all opportunities to learn something, to become better and grow. Ultimately, in every situation there is an opportunity to take shelter of the higher power of God and in doing so we find that life has inconceivable treasures in every moment. Therefore, to seek the essence means to look for the hand of God in every situation. This is the spiritual definition of success.

If we simply lament when things go wrong nothing is accomplished. But if, in a difficult situation, we sincerely take shelter of the Lord and, with our God-given ability, try to fix and improve that situation, then we can turn a curse into a blessing. The story of the greatest success in life often involves a person who hits rock-bottom only to discover something so beautiful and precious that if they didn't go through it, they would have lived a mediocre spiritual life and not have accomplished so much within.

Without gratitude, we cannot be satisfied in the heart. Whatever we get, we feel we deserve, and we want something more. And whatever we get, we feel it's expected. 'I should get this.' And when we don't get what we want, we complain and blame others, 'Why is the world against me?'

The universal principle of all spiritual paths and a very basic principle of the Shri Bhagavad Gita teaches us that we should be grateful for whatever God gives us. When good things come, we should feel, 'I don't deserve this. But I am so grateful.' We should be grateful for even a little bit of kindness that a person shows us. We should be grateful for any blessings we receive. And the difficulties, pains and failures—we should be grateful for those too, that we could learn and grow through those experiences otherwise we may have missed a precious chance. Through our challenges we can learn to come closer to God, we can improve the quality of our own lives and overcome the obstacles that hold us back. But the lessons that the Lord communicates to us from within our hearts can only be heard when there is gratitude.

THIRTY-SIX

Take Worries to God

Human Quality: Respond (Don't React)

In the holy town of Dwarka in coastal Gujarat lived Madhav, a primary-school boy. He was the youngest of three siblings. His father was a milkman and his mother was a homemaker. His elder brother had recently graduated from college and his sister was in high school.

The city of Dwarka is built around the Dwarkadish temple, which is dedicated to Lord Krishna. It was a common practice for Madhav and his family to pay a visit to the temple every Saturday. Every time the family visited the temple, Madhav left behind crumpled pieces of paper as he exited the main shrine. This happened for two weeks and the man who would clean up the temple observed this. When Madhav arrived for the third time that month, the sweeper picked the pieces of paper Madhav had dropped and took him to the priest.

The following notes were written on those pieces of paper that day:

'Meera has fever.'

'Mukund needs a job.'

'We need rent money.'

As they went to the priest and as he saw these notes, he asked Madhav, 'What is this, young boy?'

Madhav remained silent for a minute.

'Please tell me, I won't complain to your mother,' the priest assured him.

'I saw a signboard near my school,' Madhav began. 'It said: Take your worries to the temple and leave them there.'

The priest was moved by the young boy's faith in Krishna.

'So,' Madhav continued, 'I write my worries down on those little pieces of paper every Saturday morning. I pray for those worries to vanish, then I crumple them up and leave them here.'

The priest blessed Madhav well and gave him some prasadam.

In the Bhagavad Gita (7.16), it is said:

catur-vidhā bhajante māṁ
janāḥ su-kṛtino 'rjuna
ārto jijñāsur arthārthī
jñānī ca bharataraṣabha

'O best among the *Bhāratas*, four kinds of pious men begin to render devotional service unto Me—the distressed, the desirer of wealth, the inquisitive and he who is searching for knowledge of the Absolute.'

This story exemplifies the pure heart of Madhav. Despite challenges in life and the worries that engulfed his heart, he didn't get bogged down but took shelter of the Supreme Lord. Reversals in life are indeed a norm and challenges surmount us at various points in time. Such situations can happen in everyone's life. What separates the great from the rest is their response to challenging situations. They respond and do not react. One such great person, a noble king who walked our planet, was King Dasharath. Let's learn a few lessons from his glorious life.

Maharaj Dasharath, Lord Ram's father, the great monarch of Ayodhya led the heritage of his kingdom in such a way that the hearts of his citizens were always filled with the love of God and one another. There was not a tinge of dissatisfaction in their faces and no lack of opulence in their houses.

Let's look into his life to grasp some lessons in building the right attitude when adversities arise.

CHOOSE DUTY AND DETERMINATION OVER DUALITIES OF THE MATERIAL WORLD

It wasn't because King Dasharath happened to be the father of Lord Ram that he got relieved from all material miseries of life. He had 60,000 queens. Yet, he was a monarch without a son. However hard one may try, pleasure in this world is invariably mixed with pain. This is the nature of the material world.

Krishna says in the Bhagavad Gita, '*Dukhalayam açāçvatam*'. This means that the material world is a place of misery. Therefore, experiencing this dilemma, Dasharath Maharaj teaches us that even if one is living in a beautiful city like Ayodhya, the dualities of this world will surface and this is unavoidable. One must learn to perform his/her duties with resolute determination and fight against all odds.

ACCEPTING INSTRUCTIONS FROM GREAT SOULS WITH SUBMISSION

Vishwamitra Muni approached King Dasharath with a petition to send Lord Ram with him for his first assignment to kill demons. However, the king denied it and instead proposed to send his whole army. A spiritual master's instructions are for the disciple's welfare, however inconceivable they may seem. An aspiring disciple may try to avoid them if it bothers their attachment. Although here Dasharath Maharaj's loving attachment is for the Supreme Lord Ram, still the principle to be kept in mind is that when an instruction comes from a great soul one must try to follow it to the best of one's abilities, as it always results in a greater good. The reason for the disagreement is beautifully pointed out by Vishwamitra Muni, 'You cannot understand properly because you are sitting on a throne but I am sitting at the lotus feet of the Lord.'

Mahatmas hold a vision that transcends temporary gain and loss and is beyond a commoner's conception. Thus, better to serve them with obeisance and submission.

INFERIORITY COMPLEX OR HUMILITY?

Once, Maharaj Dasharath called for all Ayodhya *vasis*. In the huge assembly he asked them, 'I'm thinking of making my son Ram the king of Ayodhya. What is your opinion?' The significance of this seemingly simple anecdote is profound. Maharaj Dasharath had ruled Ayodhya for 60,000 years yet he had the humility to consult what his citizens collectively desired. The citizens responded was great enthusiasm and the assembly hall reverberated with the sound. They said it was the best decision he had taken in the last 60,000 years of his rule. Hearing this, King Dasharath felt utterly insignificant despite rendering service for such a long time. He instantly experienced the insecurity and fear of being a useless ruler, and that his service held no value to his subjects.

However, with a magnanimous heart, he requested them to let him know his faults in performing his administrative duties. The citizens discretely wrote a letter to him stating there is only one fault in you, Maharaj Dasharath—you have given birth to such a faultless son like Ram, who is an exemplary divine personality full of unlimited good qualities. That is your only fault.

Reading this, Maharaj Dasharath was relieved and merrily coronated Lord Ram as the king of Ayodhya. The principle to note here is that it is vital to differentiate between inferiority complex and humility. One emerges from false ego while the latter is due to the influence of pure devotional service.

BE CAUTIOUS WHILE PREPARING FOR THE INEVITABLE

There was one mistake that bred in the palace of Ayodhya which caused a separation between the former king and the newly coronated one, breaking the hearts of everyone in the kingdom. That was envy. Envy in the form of Manthara, the maidservant of the most favoured queen Kaikeyi. Kaikeyi was entrapped by the manipulative latches of the envious Manthara. This led to the king's inexplicable painful separation from the Supreme Lord. Dasharath had to oblige to the evil demands of his queen and send away Lord Ram to the forest. That was the end of his life.

Someone asked Srila Prabhupada, 'Why is the death rate in India increasing?'

He smiled back, 'The death rate is same everywhere at 100 per cent. One who was born has to die.'

It's interesting to note that a king like Dasharath who ruled Ayodhya for 60,000 years left his body without any of his four dear sons beside him. All of his life's dreams were shattered and his last breath was an exhale of despair due to his separation from his beloved Ram. One can never predict which way life is going to go. Thus, preparing for the inevitable death is necessary. Our journey is indeed unpredictable. Thus, it is important to be engaged in spiritual practices seriously under bona fide guidance of a spiritual master without any delay.

THIRTY-SEVEN

The Weekend Homework

Human Quality: Controlling the Mind

It was a Saturday afternoon in the hill station of Shillong. It was about time for the school to close at St Anthony's Convent School. As the school bell rang, Ronee, a ten-year-old, rushed out of the classroom. When he saw his father waiting at the gate, he picked up speed. They got into the car and started talking.

'How was the day, Ronee?' the father asked.

'Very good, Dad. It was Maya's birthday and Gagan returned to school after being out sick for the last three days. It was good fun.'

'That's great to hear. So, what did you learn today?'

'Actually, my moral-science teacher has given me an interesting homework.'

'I see,' he sighed, 'and what's that?'

'She has asked us to hug ten people and then tell each one of them, "Be patient and trust life. Besides God, I love you too."'

'Wow! That's so kind,' the father cheered. 'We will go to the mall this evening. You can begin your homework there.'

Ronee took a post-lunch nap and his spirits were high when he woke up as he looked forward to the evening. 'Let's go!' he cheered.

'As you can see here,' the father opened the windows, 'there is heavy rainfall today. I am sorry, I suspect we can't make it.'

The boy insisted and pushed him hard. Although it continued to pour, the father still drove to the mall to please his son.

They went to a few outlets in the mall and made the necessary purchases. Meanwhile, Ronee went about his pursuit of hugging people and saying those kind words. Thanks to the rain, the crowd in the mall was lower than expected and it was indeed quite a task for Ronee to find ten people.

The rain hadn't stopped yet and with a few interspersed thunderstorms, it had turned dark. Ronee's father insisted that they leave for home right away.

'Nine done, Dad,' Ronee announced. 'Just one more, please.'

'Let's leave now,' the father resisted. 'It's raining heavily, and we shouldn't get stuck. You can complete this tomorrow.'

Sad yet understanding the situation, Ronee obliged. As they were heading back, the rain had stopped. However, there was a boulder that had fallen on the street. There was a heavy traffic jam there.

Ronee looked up to find a quaint house atop a mini hill. He could see a lit candle and its beams flashing through its French windowpanes.

'That's a beautiful house up there,' Ronee pointed to it. 'Please, Dad, just one more person is remaining, let me complete my homework.'

'What do you mean?' the father asked as they waited for the traffic to clear.

'Yes, let me go up and hug the person there.'

'But . . .'

'C'mon Dad, anyway we are stuck here.'

The father gave in, pulled the car over and drove into the parking basement of that house.

Excited, Ronee climbed up the stairs and pressed the bell. Enthused, he pounded the door strongly with his knuckles.

'Wait, Ronee,' his father said, climbing up, 'Don't be in a hurry.'

After a few seconds, the door was opened gently. On the other side was a lady. Dressed in pyjamas, she looked pale and it seemed that she was in the middle of a horrid time that day.

'What can I do for you, son?' she asked Ronee.

'Maybe we have come . . .' his father began, unsure, 'at the wrong time, we are sorry.'

With radiant eyes and a bright smile, Ronee interrupted and said to the lady, 'I want to hug you.'

He hugged her tight, with a lot of warmth, and then told her, 'Be patient and trust life. Besides God, I love you too.'

The lady embraced him and started crying profusely.

Ronee's father was stumped, not knowing how to defuse the situation and get her back to normal.

Reluctantly, he asked, 'Ma'am, do you need help? Shall I fetch some water?'

She was trying to speak but her voice choked up and she was palpitating. Ronee's father quickly stepped into the house and returned with a glass of water.

She sipped the water, composed herself in a few seconds and took them inside. She took Ronee to a room filled with toys and let him play there.

'Thank you, sir, for dropping by,' she told Ronee's father as they sat together in the hall.

'Our pleasure,' he replied, still unsure of what she was going through.

'You have such a lovely son,' she said in an emotional tone.

Ronee's father smiled back.

'My husband died a few days ago,' she continued in a low tone, 'leaving me feel shattered. I feel lonely today. It's a long story but, for strange reasons, the family sees me as the reason for my husband's death. This couldn't be more ridiculous. In fact, I feel the saddest after his passing away. How could I . . .?' and she shed tears.

'That's so unfortunate,' he comforted her.

'In the last two weeks, no one has turned up to inquire about my well-being. Leave alone a visit, I did not receive a phone call nor a message. I am so depressed. Today morning my heart felt heavy, and the emotions took over me. Since morning I have been thinking that this is the end of the road for me.'

'Oh my god!' he exclaimed.

'Then I took a chair and rope to my bedroom and decided to end my life. As I was seeing the world for one last time, I begged God for forgiveness, poured my heart out to Him. Just then, I heard your knock on the door.'

It was a revelation for Ronee's father and he looked up to thank God.

'I wondered who would come and meet me and truth be told, I was in two minds whether or not to open the door.'

'I am glad you did,' he butted in.

'Yes, when I did, I couldn't believe what my eyes saw. Such a cute-looking boy. His hug and the words that he uttered moved me. Ronee's entry is God's response to my prayer.'

They talked for a while and the lady changed her mind and instead gathered the courage to look at life with positivity.

In life, we can sometimes play a very important role in making people go closer to God. We may not realize it but we do act as instruments of God. And we should strive to be one always.

In the Bhagavad Gita (12.7), Krishna says:

teṣām ahaṁ samuddhartā
mṛtyu-saṁsāra-sāgarāt
bhavāmi na cirāt pārtha
mayy āveśita-cetasām

'For those who worship Me, giving up all their activities unto Me and being devoted to Me without deviation, who are engaged in devotional service and always meditating upon Me, having fixed their minds upon Me, O son of Partha— for them I am the swift deliverer from the ocean of birth and death.'

How we control the mind is a very important aspect here. That determines whether we move closer to Krishna or get swayed by disturbances.

According to Sage Patanjali, disturbances are like the wind that blows over the chitta or consciousness. When the wind blows over the ocean of chitta, then waves are created. So, these disturbances result in five mental states or *vrittis*. It is these mental states or vrittis that can sometimes prevent us from fixing our mind on Krishna or moving closer to God.

Let us discuss these vrittis in detail. All of us fall under one of these five mental states at any given point in time:

1. *Praman*—Receiving proper knowledge

Praman is how one obtains the right kind of knowledge, either through direct experience, hypothetical reasoning or through revealed scriptures and authorities which are majorly categorized as *shabda* (authorized sources), *anumana* (historical evidence) and *pratyaksha* (sense perception). Most often, our minds acquire loads of information and knowledge through inferences, perception, experience and other means. The right kind of knowledge allows one to see things as they are without the filter of prejudices. When acquired, it brings one to the level of sobriety.

2. *Viparyay*—Error

When someone drinks alcohol, they start seeing two moons in the sky and declare that they would research and publish papers on astronomy. Such a distorted state of mind allows for faulty information to pierce through our objective sense of reality. Therefore, often we perceive information as we want it to be rather than for what it is. So, there are times when our mental state is bound to err. This state is called viparya.

3. *Vikalpa*—Imagination

This kind of imagination means something that appears to be ordinary when colloquially referred to but that which does not constitute a truth. For example, we say that the sun rises and sets. There is no problem with it. But the actual truth is, the sun neither rises nor sets. Sometimes, we say 'time flies', does this mean that time grew wings and has suddenly begun to fly? All these fall under the category of vikalpa or imagination where a certain concept is referred to only for social understanding and in speech but in reality, it doesn't represent anything factual.

4. *Nidra*—Deep sleep state

The fourth mental state is nidra. Everyone is familiar with this. Perhaps one of the most loved and sought after mental states is deep sleep. When *tamo guna* or the mode of ignorance fully overwhelms the intelligence or *buddhi*, we dive into deep sleep. When the *rajo guna* or the mode of passion mixes with this mode of ignorance, we attain the dreaming state. However, dreaming doesn't come under vritti or mental state. When there is a touch of *sattva guna* or the mode of goodness, we wake up refreshed. However, when the rajo guna or mode of passion dominates the mode of ignorance in sleep, we wake up restless. If there is only tamo guna in sleep, we wake up sluggish and feel sleepier and lazier. We experience various such combinations every time we are off to sleep.

5. *Smriti*—Memory

The fifth and most important mental state of all is memory or remembrance. Sage Patanjali beautifully defines smriti as *anubhuta visayam asmaparosa smriti*: meaning, a sensory experience that doesn't slip away. This smriti ultimately triggers the *raga* or attachment (the first mental state mentioned above) and then the cycle continues. Memories are a reactivation of imprints of the sense objects one has experienced and recognized in the past. If chitta is like a lake, then memories are like pebbles. To the extent the lake is clear, you can see the pebbles. Retrievable thoughts come under memory and those which cannot be retrieved fall under the subconscious mind.

SANSKAR—IMPRINTS

The result of these five mental states is sanskar or imprints. The experiences we go through and that which we allow to settle in our memory become a part of our vritti or mental state. There are five kleshas or disturbances which we have discussed earlier that result in five kinds of vrittis or mental states. These five kinds of vrittis influence our consciousness and create imprints which are called sanskar.

Sanskar is nothing but the imprints which are like personality traits, habits and compulsive behaviour or addictions. However, these imprints are not easily created. There is a scientific process by which the five disturbances and five mental states intricately weave our sanskar.

For example, when someone smokes, the act of smoking is stored as an imprint in the chitta. It becomes a sanskar and then it in return gets activated as desirable memory. Sanskars provoke the fourth element, which is action or karma. Klesha, vritti and sanskara provide impetus to karma. Karma can either be subha, auspicious or asubha, inauspicious.

Alternatively, it can be pious or impious. When karma or action is performed, through it a chain of actions follow. It's worth noting that at every moment, we are acting and each one of those actions is creating a series of reactions and we are repeatedly responding to those reactions, creating further actions. And this cycle goes on.

SOUL IN *SAMSARA SAGAR*—OCEAN OF MATERIAL ACTIONS

The soul cannot be inactive even for a moment. The number of actions we perform within twenty-four hours is inconceivable. Those droplets of action and reaction cumulatively form an ocean by the end of one's lifespan. That ocean of action and reaction is thus called samsara sagar. Samsara sagar is the reservoir of infinite voluminous reactions we create and it is so vast that it cannot be experienced all at once within one's lifetime. The debt is so huge that we cannot repay it in one lifetime. So, we take birth again and again. Then, as we proceed to live the next life, we are affected by the five kleshas again, which result in five mental states, then the samsara is formed and karma is recreated. To experience the reactions of karma, we take birth again in this material world.

Thus, we have to realize the strength of our impressions and the compulsive behaviour that we have adopted over several lifetimes. The practice recommended by Patanjali in his writings is to take up yoga which brings stillness and steadiness of mind to perform activities with proper consciousness.

Srila Prabhupada, the founder acharya of ISKCON Society, advocates the practice of chanting of the Hare Krishna maha mantra. Chanting of this most powerful mantra is most suited in the age we live in, Kali Yuga.

Hare Krishna Hare Krishna Krishna Krishna Hare Hare
Hare Ram Hare Ram Ram Ram Hare Hare.

It not just brings in stillness and steadiness to the mind but also help us get out of the cycle of birth and death, beyond the remit of karma.

THIRTY-EIGHT

Valuing Relationships

Human Quality: Relationships

It was a pleasant October evening in the garden city of Bangalore. Located on the Deccan Plateau at a height of over 3000 feet above sea level, the Silicon Valley of India boasts pleasant weather conditions throughout the year, barring the summer months of March–April. Even if the sun comes out in the afternoon, there are high chances of light rain that brings down the temperature by evening. Referred to as the retirement paradise of the twentieth century, the city is spotted with parks and lakes, and people cherish their evening walks with their children or sometimes even their dogs in the pleasant atmosphere.

While at the park one day, a woman sat down next to a man on a bench.

'That's my son over there,' she said, pointing to a little boy in a red sweater who was gliding down the slide.

'He's a fine-looking boy,' the man said. 'That's my daughter on the bike in the white dress.'

Then, looking at his watch, he called to his daughter. 'What do you say? Shall we go, Melissa?'

Melissa pleaded, 'Just five more minutes, Dad. Please! Just five more minutes.'

The man nodded and Melissa continued to ride her bike to her heart's content. Minutes passed and the father stood and called again to his daughter. 'Time to go now?'

Again, Melissa pleaded, 'Five more minutes, Dad. Just five more minutes.'

The man smiled and said, 'OK.'

This went on a couple more times.

'My god,' the lady exclaimed, 'you certainly are a patient father.'

'Well, maybe,' the man smiled. 'Her elder brother Tommy was killed by a drunk driver last year while he was riding his bike near here.'

'My god! I'm sorry to hear that,' the lady replied.

'I never spent much time with Tommy,' the man continued, 'and now I'd give anything for just five more minutes with him. I've vowed not to make the same mistake with Melissa. She thinks she has five more minutes to ride her bike. The truth is, I get five more minutes to watch her play.'

Life is all about your priorities and family is a top priority compared to most others, so let us invest our time in our loved ones.

The *Srimad Bhagavatam* (7.2.21) says:

bhūtānām iha saṁvāsaḥ
prapāyām iva suvrate
daivenaikatra nītānām
unnītānāṁ sva-karmabhiḥ

My dear mother, in a restaurant or place for drinking cold water, many travellers are brought together, and after drinking water they continue to their respective destinations. Similarly, living entities join in a family and later, because of their own actions, they are led apart to their destinations.

This verse presents a realistic portrayal of family life in the material world and it's very important that we build a correct understanding and interpretation of it. This can also be compared to a train journey where we come together with fellow passengers for a definite period, spanning a few hours or days. Life in the material world is similar but for a much more elongated period, spanning years and decades.

There is a similar verse in the Bhagavad Gita (3.27):

> *prakṛteḥ kriyamāṇāni*
> *guṇaiḥ karmāṇi sarvaśaḥ*
> *ahaṅkāra-vimūḍhātmā*
> *kartāham iti manyate*

'The bewildered soul, under the influence of the three modes of material nature, thinks himself the doer of activities, which are in actuality carried out by nature.'

Fundamentally, we are souls, we are spiritual beings who belong to the spiritual world. All of us, living entities in this material world, have come here only because we wanted to be equal to God, Krishna and enjoy being independent of him. Hence, we have been sent here to be conditioned by material nature in different degrees. All living entities act exactly according to the directions of *prakâti*, material nature, because in the material world we are fully under a higher control.

The material world we live in can be compared to a prison, and harsh as it may sound, the family is a combination of several individuals placed in a home to fulfil the terms of their imprisonment. As the prisoners scatter as soon as their terms are over and they are released, all of us who have temporarily assembled as family members will continue to our respective destinations.

However, because of our material conditioning, we get attached to the family members we are in the company of and moments like suffering or the death of a loved one cause us deep suffering. Another example given is that family members are like straws carried together by the waves of a river. Sometimes such straws mix together in whirlpools and later, dispersed again by the same waves, they float alone in the water.

While such examples are provided in the scriptures to help us understand the temporary nature of the material world and the associated harsh reality of separation with family members at some point of time, this should not be misconstrued as encouraging an indifferent outlook towards family members. In fact, we should view every living being (including animals, reptiles, plants, insects, etc) as individual souls and as part and parcel of God. That way, we view the world as one family, *Vasudhaiva Kutumbakam*. And we don't restrict our love and care to our so-called family members but extend it to the world at large and with Krishna at the centre, serve everyone in a way that pleases them.

To help us inculcate this thought process in life, practising seven types of social collaboration could be a starting point. These is highly recommended for happiness in our social dealings:

1. **Be generous to relatives**

   A good starting point is to begin looking beyond one's immediate family (parents, spouse and children) and to be generous to relatives. Be generous to them by expressing care and love, and in terms of sincerity of service whenever an opportunity arises and also offer financial help whenever they are in need. That way, we become more broad-minded.

2. **Be kind to strangers**

   Looking beyond one's relatives to include strangers is the next step. Sometimes people have a habit to restrict their kindness to people they are associated with. However, being kind (especially when in need) to even people we don't know is important as it reduces attachment to family members and at the same time broadens our worldview.

3. **Be cunning with the wicked**

   As they say, 'As you sow, so shall you reap'. When we deal with the wicked, it's important that we respond appropriately. This is to be seen as a situational response and not as a blanket response that is being encouraged. By being cunning and giving the wicked a taste of their own medicine, we navigate a potential trap and at the same time, communicate emphatically that we have a no-nonsense approach towards untoward behaviour.

4. **Be loving to the good**

   In contrast to the above, we should be loving to the good. That way, we also send across a message that their goodness is deeply appreciated and that we would reciprocate with more love. This expression of love can have a ripple effect as such good people feel encouraged and continue to be good to others. This can go a long way in nurturing good behaviour globally.

5. **Be frank with the learned**

   'Learned' not only refers to individual who have acquired an education on material matters but also people who have acquired knowledge on spiritual topics. With the spiritually learned, it's important that we don't manipulate our conversations and be frank in our portrayal of things. That's because they have the potency and wisdom to look right through us and gauge our intent. When we are frank, they appreciate our honesty and earnestly share their knowledge with us and help us learn and evolve as individuals.

6. **Be valorous towards the enemy**

   Along the lines of being cunning with the wicked, one needs to take one's interactions head-on with the enemy. When there is threat of attack, one needs to proactively prepare to respond to it. Vedic scriptures authorize violence in the context of self-defence.

7. **Be patient with elders**

   As the body ages, weakening happens not just physically but mentally too. As a result, as people get older, their grasping power can weaken and their ability to communicate succinctly can take a beating. On the contrary, youngsters are bubbling with energy and the mind operates at breakneck speed. With this understanding, we should be more empathetic towards elders and be patient for them to operate at the speed that they are able to.

If we can apply these seven types of social collaborations effectively, we can make gradual progress in our spiritual life and not be too attached materially.

THIRTY-NINE

Challenge Helps Growth

Human Quality: Self-Development

Along the shores of the Morna river in Vidarbha lived a saint who took shelter in a Laxmi Narayan temple. The saint always spent time chanting the holy names of God and prayed for the welfare of the inhabitants of the village. This was a small village in the Akola district in Maharashtra. It was customary practice for the villagers to visit the temple daily. The temple was a centre point of sorts and villagers used this as a public place to meet neighbours.

Often, they also engaged in conversations on the deep philosophical matters with the saint. And occasionally, on a request basis, the saint would deliver discourses on the Bhagavad Gita, the Puranas and the epics like the Mahabharata and the Ramayana prior to festivals like Ram Navami, Krishna Janmashtami, etc. The saint led a simple life, reading from the Vedic scriptures and taking remnants of the bhoga (sanctified food) offered to Shri Laxmi Narayan daily. On festival days or special occasions, the residents voluntarily served the saint the feast cooked at their place.

In the same village lived Kuldeep, a college-going youth, with his parents and sister. Kuldeep was studious, scientific in thinking and not fond of spiritual topics. Rather, he viewed religion as divisive and found it a waste of time in the modern era. Besides, he felt that the saint was doing no work and simply whiling away time eating free food offered by the temple and the villagers. He also didn't like the people thronging the temple for group discussions with the saint or attending his discourses. This feeling lingered in Kuldeep for a long time. But, after a few years, as he aged, gained maturity and confidence, he realized the need to challenge the saint and make him learn a lesson for his supposed inactiveness.

So, Kuldeep started attending sessions in the evening when residents would discuss philosophical matters with the saint. These were small groups of people, ranging from five to seven members. Inquisitive, they would question the saint on some of the Vedic principles, the basis of the caste system, etc. Whenever the saint used to explain a topic or elaborated on a point, Kuldeep would contradict the saint, challenge, question and sometimes even confront him. This went on for a while and fellow members wondered why he was doing so every single time without factoring in logic sometimes. When they advised Kuldeep to be more broad-minded and be receptive to the words of the saint, Kuldeep would retort saying that religion is fundamentally narrow-minded and that his very purpose of challenging the saint was to make him as well as the audience broad-minded.

Although Kuldeep didn't change his behaviour, the saint never retaliated and also always maintained his composure. Even when Kuldeep wouldn't let him complete a sentence, the saint would patiently hear him out and then continue. He would even tolerate insults, not take any offence from the confrontation and instead take it in a positive spirit. Months passed by and Kuldeep's attacks on the saint only increased, both in intensity and frequency.

One Sunday afternoon, there was news in the village that Kuldeep had died in a road accident. On his way back home from a friend's house, his bike was knocked down by a state transport bus and he had died on the spot. The villagers gathered at his house and within no time, the saint also reached his house where his body was kept. Kuldeep's friends looked remorseful and sang praises of his sharp intellect and went back in time discussing childhood days. They also noticed that the saint looked equally morose and pensive.

One of Kuldeep's friends asked the saint, 'As his friends, we are sad. But why are you looking so sad and morose?'

'Why not?' the saint quipped.

'No, but,' the friend added, confused, 'Kuldeep would always confront you, challenge you.'

'Yes, he did,' the saint calmly replied.

'But,' another friend chimed in, 'it looks like you are deeply, genuinely grieving his departure.'

'Yes I am,' the saint affirmed. 'And actually, I feel sad for myself.'

'But why?' asked the first friend. 'In fact, you must be angry with him.'

'Not at all. Kuldeep would always challenge me and confront me. His challenges and confrontations would force me to go deep within myself, contemplate on his arguments, read the scriptures more deeply and think of ways to improve myself.'

The friends looked puzzled.

The saint continued, 'Now the question is, in his absence who will push me to improve myself further. Therefore I feel extremely sad.'

The friends were amazed by his response.

'I did not see Kuldeep as someone who was against me. I would see his challenges and questioning of me as an opportunity for me to grow.'

Kuldeep's friends folded their hands in awe of the saint's mindset.

In the *Srimad Bhagavatam* (10.20.16) it is said:

> *mārgā babhūvuḥ sandigdhās*
> *tṛṇaiś channā hy asaṁskṛtāḥ*
> *nābhyasyamānāḥ śrutayo*
> *dvijaiḥ kālena cāhatāḥ*

'When we do not spend sufficient time improving ourselves, in due course of time our hearts and minds will be covered by the grass of illusion, just like a village path is covered by grass and debris in the rainy season.'

The mindset with which we approach challenges in life is very important. We should view them as opportunities for growth.

Focusing on self-development makes us look forward to a higher goal in life and, essentially, makes our life purposeful. We should view self-development as a pole star, i.e., no matter the situation that comes upon us, if we focus on self-development, we naturally view every challenge as a growth opportunity and lead a purposeful life.

Here are six tips to lead a life centred on self-development.

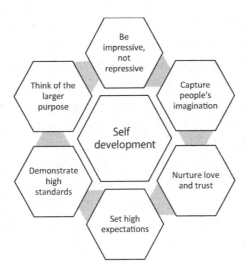

1. **Be impressive, not repressive**

   Remaining positive and positioning oneself with a service attitude is important. We don't need to be in a mode to impress others. If we always think about how we can create a positive difference in the lives of people around us, that is success in life. Sometimes we tend to be insecure and exercise control in such a way that it restricts people. That breaks relationships and trust between people. Specifically, for those in leadership positions, empowering people, their team members is important.

2. **Capture people's imagination with positive behaviour**

   An impactful way to capture people's imagination, in other words, make them feel excited about your company is by being positive. If we can transmit positive vibes by being encouraging, collaborative and receptive and listening actively, we let them know that we value them. Even when we share our perspectives or give direction to people as leaders, we can be welcoming of their inputs and not be dogmatic. That makes people look up to us and appreciate our views.

3. **Nurture love and trust among the people in your charge**
   As leaders, we should understand that we are trustees of our team members' welfare: both personal well-being and professional development. Some leaders tend to exercise control over team members, and it backfires. Such a tendency stems from insecurity and lack of confidence in one's leadership capability. If we see ourselves as trustees, we care for their well-being and hence nurture love. As a result, an environment of trust develops between team members

4. **Set high expectations from team members**
   While leaders continue to remain trustees of our team members' well-being, they have a responsibility to facilitate their growth and development.

   Setting high expectations from team members and constantly finding ways to get them out of their comfort zone are good starting points. Radical candour, as it is called, is a behaviour that leaders should exhibit. It's the ability where leaders challenge team members directly when they care for them personally. Such leaders may come across as insensitive but they remain kind.

5. **Demonstrate high standards**
   As leaders set high expectations from their team, they accomplish desired results only when they walk the talk,

by demonstrating those high standards in their own work. When leaders demonstrate what that 'high' standard is through action, the team members receive direction accordingly and can emulate the same. By walking the talk, leaders earn the respect of team members and they are seen as being more hands-on and technically competent. That helps them be more empathetic and guide their team members well.

6. **Think of the larger purpose**

   We tend to go with the flow and get into the thick of things without being mindful of what they all lead to. It's important to constantly evaluate what we are up to, assess the larger impact of our action and the larger purpose we contribute to. It's not just enough to realize this, we should also communicate this to our team members to inspire them. That way, their self-development journey will also be purposeful.

FORTY

Whom to Be?

Human Quality: Satisfaction

There was once a stonecutter who felt dissatisfied most of the time. He experienced an emptiness within. There was a lack of contentment in his life and he always found something missing in him. Over time, he got used to comparison and always thought he was on a weak footing, that many others were more gifted than he was.

A few days passed and as he was sawing wood, he watched a wealthy merchant pass by in his car. One look at his opulence and the kind of attention this wealthy merchant was drawing, he developed a desire, 'How I wish I was as rich! I should become a rich, wealthy, powerful like he is.'

A few weeks passed and there was a procession one day right outside the stonecutter's house. He observed that this procession was led by many musicians and a group of people were holding someone on a palanquin. The stonecutter looked inside carefully and he saw a government official. The officer displayed his power, influence and position in full glory. In a few moments, the stonecutter saw that many wealthy merchants had come to the road and offered taxes to this government official.

The stonecutter developed another desire, 'Maybe I should become a government official. He is more powerful than a wealthy merchant. This way, I will become more satisfied.'

A few minutes passed and then this government official felt suffocated by the heavy coat that he was wearing as he was walking on the road. It was the onset of the summer and the sun was blaring heat.

The stonecutter looked at the sun and thought, 'Oh! Looks like the sun is more powerful than the government official. Maybe I should become like the sun.'

A few days passed, and as his goalpost changed, a group of black clouds covered the sun one humid afternoon. After a week of sweltering heat, the clouds had taken over and it began to pour heavily.

The stonecutter wondered, 'Oh! How powerful are the clouds! They have overpowered the sun. I should become like the clouds. That will make me satisfied.'

Later that evening, a gust of wind blew and the clouds dispersed. Looking away from his work to the sky, the stonecutter shifted his goalpost yet again, 'Maybe it's the wind that overpowers all.'

Just as he was thinking this way, he noticed the large mountain some distance away. Although he could experience the wind gushing by, the mountain remained sturdy, unmoving. Then, he thought, 'Oh! The rocky mountain is more powerful than the wind.'

He looked down at the bottom of the mountain and noticed another stonecutter who was chipping apart stones. He took a closer look and saw that this stonecutter was breaking rocks from this gigantic mountain.

'Oh! Looks like a stonecutter is more powerful than even a rocky mountain.'

In the Bhagavad Gita (2.65), Lord Krishna says:

> *prasāde sarva-duḥkhānāṁ*
> *hānir asyopajāyate*
> *prasanna-cetaso hy āśu*
> *buddhiḥ paryavatiṣṭhate*

Amongst all kinds of powers available in this world, the greatest power is the power of satisfaction. When one is flooded with that power of satisfaction from within, sarva-duhkhanam hanir, one rises above the sense of insecurity, insufficiency and fear. This feeling of satisfaction is the real power which makes a person feel at peace within. One feels blissful no matter the kind of situation one is surrounded by. Let us try to experience this great power by connecting with the real satisfaction within.

The journey towards satisfaction begins with understanding the equation to happiness. The ESCAPE acronym can be a guiding light to achieve satisfaction.

E: Give up unreasonable EXPECTATIONS

While at a restaurant, we may order a dosa or pizza as per our desire, but once we are in a hospital, we cannot place a similar order, 'Doctor! Two syringes, fast!'

A hospital is a place where we are helpless and with folded hands, we appeal to the doctors, 'Whatever you say is OK with me. I surrender.'

śādhi mām tvām prapannam

The Bhagavad Gita provides a unique solution to each individual, just as doctors treat each patient differently according to their disease. Out of all unreasonable expectations, 'I'm the controller of my life' is the topmost. It is due to the envy of the supreme controller, God, and this is the root cause of our miserable existence. This perennially blocks us from experiencing infinite bliss. Because of the *ahankār* or false ego, we think we are the controllers and develop a sense of proprietorship. Eventually, such a desire and its expectation merge into frustration, leading to the next stage called anger, *kāma esa krodha esa*.

S: Follow the right definition is SUCCESS

Life is a process and not a product. To achieve the right understanding of success, we must have the right guidance. The right definition of success is not only to get the best but to give the best. In the 1936 Berlin Olympics, Hitler had one agenda, to prove that Germans were the best. Jesse Owens, an Afro-American represented the USA in the long jump. Hitler wanted to defeat him at all costs. Owens was constantly jumping beyond the marked line. So, Luz Long, the German athlete chosen by Hitler, came to Owens, put his hand on his shoulder and gave him tips on adjusting his jump to qualify. Even though Long had political backing and was competing against Owens, he showed comradeship and helped a fellow competitor. Later, Owens won gold and made the world record of 8.06 metres which stood unbeatable for the next twenty-five years. He said, 'Even if you melt all my gold medals, it will not equate to even a single plating of the 24-carat friendship that I had with Luz Long.'

Achievement cannot bring happiness. Only the genuine bonds we create can provide us with true fulfilment of heart. Thus, the definition of success is not external but internal.

C: Give up unhealthy COMPARISON

His Holiness Radhanath Swami often quotes, 'False ego is the foundation of the house. You cannot see it, but it is supporting the whole house.' So, the material existence is a product of our false ego. When pride comes, one has already fallen. Whatever happens after that is simply a detail of one's fallen condition. Many other religions teach people how to give up sin. But Srila Prabhupada taught how to give up the root cause of sin, which is false ego. Ultimately, all comparisons centre around false ego and false identity.

We tend to express ourselves as superior to others. This breeds envy. Envy is an indirect form of appreciation. Unless we find something valuable in others, we will not feel envious of them. We should therefore overcome envy and directly appreciate the thing we envy in someone.

Television and social media have fed us unhealthy ideals to compare ourselves with. We ruin our self-worth because of another unique individual going about their life with a different pursuit altogether. That is foolishness. We should simply draw inspiration from others. A healthier practice is to compare our past and present versions for our betterment. That is the growth mindset.

A: APPRECIATE and ACCEPT what God has given

It is estimated that more than 4 million people around the globe are suffering from some kind of phobia. So, if you woke up today without any pain or fear, be grateful. Appreciating what God has given is an important factor in finding happiness in everything he has provided us. Depression will cease to exist if we express gratitude for everything we have rather than worrying about what we lack. If your basic needs are covered, you are richer than 75 per cent of the world population because the rest of them are dying of hunger. If you have some savings, you belong to the top 10 per cent who constitute a prosperous section of society.

Moreover, if you have never known the danger of loneliness in a prison cell, take a moment to appreciate your luxury because you are safer than 500 million who are suffering in such circumstances.

Thus, whatever situation we are in, we should try to tolerate and find ways to overcome it rather than complaining or comparing it with others. God created this world for us to be content with regardless of the provisions. We should appreciate the beauty of creation. Seeing and accepting every situation, be it favourable or not, as the Lord's mercy can help us learn the right lessons.

P: Live to be PRINCIPLED

Once during a morning walk, Srila Prabhupada asked Dr Patel what he did first thing in the morning.

'I take my breakfast,' he answered.

'Even pigs do that,' Srila Prabhupada responded, leaving Dr Patel shocked.

Then, Srila Prabhupada advised him to remember and chant the holy names of God who gave him breakfast that day. Discipline and having principles in one's life adds the structure we need for spiritual progress. Yet, the principles can be challenging to update but improvements according to time, place and circumstance are required.

Principles are there to help us evaluate the right lane to take to reach our goal. But one should not have the feeling of being tied up by rules and regulations. Even kites are tied up, but they do fly high, such ropes are not binding but help us explore our freedom without being harmed. Thus, principles help us transcend to a new sense of freedom and happiness. This comes by regulating our senses and mind which may otherwise run wild and cause perplexities.

E: ENDURE difficulties

A cake recipe has whole wheat flour, sugar, baking soda, baking powder, some flavourings, etc. added to it. All of them individually taste unbearable. But once all ingredients come together, the result steals the hearts of everyone who tastes it. Similarly, when many difficult situations arise, one may find them all bitter and hard to experience. These circumstances are provided by God as ingredients to aid us in building a future that will help us endure those moments with tolerance and patience.

The concept of gaining strength comes from facing resistance:

- You gain physical strength by facing physical resistance
- You gain mental strength by resisting desires
- You gain spiritual strength by tolerating difficulties

Thus, by practising these six factors with the acronym ESCAPE, we can all easily escape the conceived miseries in our minds and develop satisfaction in life.

Acknowledgements

Writing this book has been a learning experience. It was not a single man's work. A lot of people inspired me, guided me and supported me during the course of this journey. I wish to express my heartfelt gratitude to those wonderful souls who were part of making this book happen, especially for the wisdom and the lessons that are a part of every story.

My gratitude to His Divine Grace, Srila A.C. Bhaktivedanta Swami Prabhupada, the founder acharya of ISKCON, for publishing the essence of Vedic literatures, the Bhagavad Gita and the *Srimad Bhagavatam*, published by the Bhaktivedanta Book Trust International (BBT) in multiple languages, thus making the ancient Vedic wisdom accessible to all.

My gratitude to H.H. Radhanath Swami Maharaja for his guidance over three decades and for facilitating my connection with Srila Prabhupada and ISKCON.

My heartfelt respect to H.H. Bhakti Rasamrita Swami Maharaja for introducing the concepts of Bhagavad Gita to me in my student days.

My gratitude to my father, Mr A.K. Sitaraman (Achyut Jagannatha Das) and my mother, Mrs Kalpakam Sitaraman (Sri Sachidevi Dasi) for nurturing my life with stories on spiritual wisdom and for being excellent examples of a stable and emotionally warm family, which created the foundation for absorbing the teachings of Vedic Sanatana Dharma.

I wish to offer my loving respect and feelings of gratitude to my senior leaders in ISKCON who have been the source of inspiration for me to live life following the teachings of the

Srimad Bhagawatam and share stories of spiritual lessons with the world:

H.H. Gopal Krishna Goswami Maharaja, H.H. Jayapataka Swami Maharaja, H.H. Bhakti Charu Swami Maharaja, H.H. Bhanu Swami Maharaja, H.H. Niranjana Swami Maharaja, H.H. Badrinarayana Swami Maharaja, H.H. Radha Govinda Goswami Maharaja, H.H. Sivarama Swami Maharaja, H.H. Bhakti Tirtha Swami Maharaja, H.H. Tamal Krishna Goswami Maharaja, H.H. Satsvarupa Das Goswami Maharaja, H.G. Bhurijana Prabhu, H.G. Shyamasundar Prabhu and many other disciples of Srila Prabhupada.

I acknowledge the wisdom I gained from many in the ashram, including Govinda Prabhu, Radha Gopinatha Prabhu, Shyamananda Prabhu, Sanatkumar Prabhu, Radheshyam Prabhu and Sankirtan Prabhu.

I have been highly inspired by the books, lectures and association of Shikshashtakam Prabhu, Gaurgopal Prabhu, Vrajavihari Prabhu, Chaitanya Charan Prabhu, Shubh Vilas Prabhu and Sutapa Prabhu, and acknowledge them for igniting many inspiring thoughts in me.

My special thanks to Suhail Mathur of the Book Bakers and Gurveen Chadha of Penguin Random House India for their patient and expert guidance, and intervention to craft the final version of the book.

My gratitude to the team of Ananda Caitanya Prabhu, Dr Sumanta Rudra, Gauranga Darshan Prabhu and the Bhaktivedanta Research Center (BRC) team for their support and help.

My gratitude to Rajesh Sridhar for his diligent work on every aspect of the book, including help on proofreading and editing.

Scan QR code to access the
Penguin Random House India website